C-1534   CAREER EXAMINATION SERIES

This is your
PASSBOOK for...

Water Superintendent

Test Preparation Study Guide
Questions & Answers

COPYRIGHT NOTICE

This book is SOLELY intended for, is sold ONLY to, and its use is RESTRICTED to individual, bona fide applicants or candidates who qualify by virtue of having seriously filed applications for appropriate license, certificate, professional and/or promotional advancement, higher school matriculation, scholarship, or other legitimate requirements of education and/or governmental authorities.

This book is NOT intended for use, class instruction, tutoring, training, duplication, copying, reprinting, excerption, or adaptation, etc., by:

1) Other publishers
2) Proprietors and/or Instructors of "Coaching" and/or Preparatory Courses
3) Personnel and/or Training Divisions of commercial, industrial, and governmental organizations
4) Schools, colleges, or universities and/or their departments and staffs, including teachers and other personnel
5) Testing Agencies or Bureaus
6) Study groups which seek by the purchase of a single volume to copy and/or duplicate and/or adapt this material for use by the group as a whole without having purchased individual volumes for each of the members of the group
7) Et al.

Such persons would be in violation of appropriate Federal and State statutes.

PROVISION OF LICENSING AGREEMENTS – Recognized educational, commercial, industrial, and governmental institutions and organizations, and others legitimately engaged in educational pursuits, including training, testing, and measurement activities, may address request for a licensing agreement to the copyright owners, who will determine whether, and under what conditions, including fees and charges, the materials in this book may be used them. In other words, a licensing facility exists for the legitimate use of the material in this book on other than an individual basis. However, it is asseverated and affirmed here that the material in this book CANNOT be used without the receipt of the express permission of such a licensing agreement from the Publishers. Inquiries re licensing should be addressed to the company, attention rights and permissions department.

All rights reserved, including the right of reproduction in whole or in part, in any form or by any means, electronic or mechanical, including photocopying, recording, or by any information storage and retrieval system, without permission in writing from the Publisher.

Copyright © 2025 by
National Learning Corporation

212 Michael Drive, Syosset, NY 11791
(516) 921-8888 • www.passbooks.com
E-mail: info@passbooks.com

PASSBOOK® SERIES

THE *PASSBOOK® SERIES* has been created to prepare applicants and candidates for the ultimate academic battlefield – the examination room.

At some time in our lives, each and every one of us may be required to take an examination – for validation, matriculation, admission, qualification, registration, certification, or licensure.

Based on the assumption that every applicant or candidate has met the basic formal educational standards, has taken the required number of courses, and read the necessary texts, the *PASSBOOK® SERIES* furnishes the one special preparation which may assure passing with confidence, instead of failing with insecurity. Examination questions – together with answers – are furnished as the basic vehicle for study so that the mysteries of the examination and its compounding difficulties may be eliminated or diminished by a sure method.

This book is meant to help you pass your examination provided that you qualify and are serious in your objective.

The entire field is reviewed through the huge store of content information which is succinctly presented through a provocative and challenging approach – the question-and-answer method.

A climate of success is established by furnishing the correct answers at the end of each test.

You soon learn to recognize types of questions, forms of questions, and patterns of questioning. You may even begin to anticipate expected outcomes.

You perceive that many questions are repeated or adapted so that you can gain acute insights, which may enable you to score many sure points.

You learn how to confront new questions, or types of questions, and to attack them confidently and work out the correct answers.

You note objectives and emphases, and recognize pitfalls and dangers, so that you may make positive educational adjustments.

Moreover, you are kept fully informed in relation to new concepts, methods, practices, and directions in the field.

You discover that you are actually taking the examination all the time: you are preparing for the examination by "taking" an examination, not by reading extraneous and/or supererogatory textbooks.

In short, this PASSBOOK®, used directedly, should be an important factor in helping you to pass your test.

WATER SUPERINTENDENT

DUTIES

Plans and directs the construction of new water system installations, and the reconstruction and maintenance of existing water system services and operating facilities; plans and coordinates water system projects and programs with other city and public and private activities and functions; plans and directs the business and finance management activities; prepares budget estimates and directs the maintenance of budget control; directs the preparation of specifications for, and recommends the purchase of machinery, materials, tools and other supplies; analyzes industrial. and population trends, building activity and potential fire protection needs in planning for present and future water supply; attends meetings and conferences to assist in formulating policy and to recommend improved procedures relating to the administration of the water system; reviews and adjusts complaints regarding water system activities and projects; directs the preparation and maintenance of a variety of activity, cost analysis, personnel, financial, statistical, and related records and reports; exercises administrative supervision over a wide variety of water system construction, maintenance, operations, engineering, purification and business management activities.

SCOPE OF THE EXAMINATION

The multiple-choice written test will cover knowledge, skills, and/or abilities in such areas as:

1. Construction and maintenance of water distribution systems and fire hydrants, including safety practices;
2. Planning, design and estimates for water distribution systems, including elementary hydraulics;
3. Construction, maintenance and operation of water and sewage systems, including treatment plants and pump;
4. Administrative Supervision;
5. Understanding and interpreting technical information and construction site plans;
6. Scheduling work and equipment; and
7. Preparation of written material.

HOW TO TAKE A TEST

I. YOU MUST PASS AN EXAMINATION

A. WHAT EVERY CANDIDATE SHOULD KNOW

Examination applicants often ask us for help in preparing for the written test. What can I study in advance? What kinds of questions will be asked? How will the test be given? How will the papers be graded?

As an applicant for a civil service examination, you may be wondering about some of these things. Our purpose here is to suggest effective methods of advance study and to describe civil service examinations.

Your chances for success on this examination can be increased if you know how to prepare. Those "pre-examination jitters" can be reduced if you know what to expect. You can even experience an adventure in good citizenship if you know why civil service exams are given.

B. WHY ARE CIVIL SERVICE EXAMINATIONS GIVEN?

Civil service examinations are important to you in two ways. As a citizen, you want public jobs filled by employees who know how to do their work. As a job seeker, you want a fair chance to compete for that job on an equal footing with other candidates. The best-known means of accomplishing this two-fold goal is the competitive examination.

Exams are widely publicized throughout the nation. They may be administered for jobs in federal, state, city, municipal, town or village governments or agencies.

Any citizen may apply, with some limitations, such as the age or residence of applicants. Your experience and education may be reviewed to see whether you meet the requirements for the particular examination. When these requirements exist, they are reasonable and applied consistently to all applicants. Thus, a competitive examination may cause you some uneasiness now, but it is your privilege and safeguard.

C. HOW ARE CIVIL SERVICE EXAMS DEVELOPED?

Examinations are carefully written by trained technicians who are specialists in the field known as "psychological measurement," in consultation with recognized authorities in the field of work that the test will cover. These experts recommend the subject matter areas or skills to be tested; only those knowledges or skills important to your success on the job are included. The most reliable books and source materials available are used as references. Together, the experts and technicians judge the difficulty level of the questions.

Test technicians know how to phrase questions so that the problem is clearly stated. Their ethics do not permit "trick" or "catch" questions. Questions may have been tried out on sample groups, or subjected to statistical analysis, to determine their usefulness.

Written tests are often used in combination with performance tests, ratings of training and experience, and oral interviews. All of these measures combine to form the best-known means of finding the right person for the right job.

II. HOW TO PASS THE WRITTEN TEST

A. NATURE OF THE EXAMINATION

To prepare intelligently for civil service examinations, you should know how they differ from school examinations you have taken. In school you were assigned certain definite pages to read or subjects to cover. The examination questions were quite detailed and usually emphasized memory. Civil service exams, on the other hand, try to discover your present ability to perform the duties of a position, plus your potentiality to learn these duties. In other words, a civil service exam attempts to predict how successful you will be. Questions cover such a broad area that they cannot be as minute and detailed as school exam questions.

In the public service similar kinds of work, or positions, are grouped together in one "class." This process is known as *position-classification*. All the positions in a class are paid according to the salary range for that class. One class title covers all of these positions, and they are all tested by the same examination.

B. FOUR BASIC STEPS

1) Study the announcement

How, then, can you know what subjects to study? Our best answer is: "Learn as much as possible about the class of positions for which you've applied." The exam will test the knowledge, skills and abilities needed to do the work.

Your most valuable source of information about the position you want is the official exam announcement. This announcement lists the training and experience qualifications. Check these standards and apply only if you come reasonably close to meeting them.

The brief description of the position in the examination announcement offers some clues to the subjects which will be tested. Think about the job itself. Review the duties in your mind. Can you perform them, or are there some in which you are rusty? Fill in the blank spots in your preparation.

Many jurisdictions preview the written test in the exam announcement by including a section called "Knowledge and Abilities Required," "Scope of the Examination," or some similar heading. Here you will find out specifically what fields will be tested.

2) Review your own background

Once you learn in general what the position is all about, and what you need to know to do the work, ask yourself which subjects you already know fairly well and which need improvement. You may wonder whether to concentrate on improving your strong areas or on building some background in your fields of weakness. When the announcement has specified "some knowledge" or "considerable knowledge," or has used adjectives like "beginning principles of…" or "advanced … methods," you can get a clue as to the number and difficulty of questions to be asked in any given field. More questions, and hence broader coverage, would be included for those subjects which are more important in the work. Now weigh your strengths and weaknesses against the job requirements and prepare accordingly.

3) Determine the level of the position

Another way to tell how intensively you should prepare is to understand the level of the job for which you are applying. Is it the entering level? In other words, is this the position in which beginners in a field of work are hired? Or is it an intermediate or advanced level? Sometimes this is indicated by such words as "Junior" or "Senior" in the class title. Other jurisdictions use Roman numerals to designate the level – Clerk I, Clerk II, for example. The word "Supervisor" sometimes appears in the title. If the level is not indicated by the title, check the description of duties. Will you be working under very close supervision, or will you have responsibility for independent decisions in this work?

4) Choose appropriate study materials

Now that you know the subjects to be examined and the relative amount of each subject to be covered, you can choose suitable study materials. For beginning level jobs, or even advanced ones, if you have a pronounced weakness in some aspect of your training, read a modern, standard textbook in that field. Be sure it is up to date and has general coverage. Such books are normally available at your library, and the librarian will be glad to help you locate one. For entry-level positions, questions of appropriate difficulty are chosen – neither highly advanced questions, nor those too simple. Such questions require careful thought but not advanced training.

If the position for which you are applying is technical or advanced, you will read more advanced, specialized material. If you are already familiar with the basic principles of your field, elementary textbooks would waste your time. Concentrate on advanced textbooks and technical periodicals. Think through the concepts and review difficult problems in your field.

These are all general sources. You can get more ideas on your own initiative, following these leads. For example, training manuals and publications of the government agency which employs workers in your field can be useful, particularly for technical and professional positions. A letter or visit to the government department involved may result in more specific study suggestions, and certainly will provide you with a more definite idea of the exact nature of the position you are seeking.

III. KINDS OF TESTS

Tests are used for purposes other than measuring knowledge and ability to perform specified duties. For some positions, it is equally important to test ability to make adjustments to new situations or to profit from training. In others, basic mental abilities not dependent on information are essential. Questions which test these things may not appear as pertinent to the duties of the position as those which test for knowledge and information. Yet they are often highly important parts of a fair examination. For very general questions, it is almost impossible to help you direct your study efforts. What we can do is to point out some of the more common of these general abilities needed in public service positions and describe some typical questions.

1) General information

Broad, general information has been found useful for predicting job success in some kinds of work. This is tested in a variety of ways, from vocabulary lists to questions about current events. Basic background in some field of work, such as sociology or economics, may be sampled in a group of questions. Often these are principles which have become familiar to most persons through exposure rather than through formal training. It is difficult to advise you how to study for these questions; being alert to the world around you is our best suggestion.

2) Verbal ability

An example of an ability needed in many positions is verbal or language ability. Verbal ability is, in brief, the ability to use and understand words. Vocabulary and grammar tests are typical measures of this ability. Reading comprehension or paragraph interpretation questions are common in many kinds of civil service tests. You are given a paragraph of written material and asked to find its central meaning.

3) Numerical ability

Number skills can be tested by the familiar arithmetic problem, by checking paired lists of numbers to see which are alike and which are different, or by interpreting charts and graphs. In the latter test, a graph may be printed in the test booklet which you are asked to use as the basis for answering questions.

4) Observation

A popular test for law-enforcement positions is the observation test. A picture is shown to you for several minutes, then taken away. Questions about the picture test your ability to observe both details and larger elements.

5) Following directions

In many positions in the public service, the employee must be able to carry out written instructions dependably and accurately. You may be given a chart with several columns, each column listing a variety of information. The questions require you to carry out directions involving the information given in the chart.

6) Skills and aptitudes

Performance tests effectively measure some manual skills and aptitudes. When the skill is one in which you are trained, such as typing or shorthand, you can practice. These tests are often very much like those given in business school or high school courses. For many of the other skills and aptitudes, however, no short-time preparation can be made. Skills and abilities natural to you or that you have developed throughout your lifetime are being tested.

Many of the general questions just described provide all the data needed to answer the questions and ask you to use your reasoning ability to find the answers. Your best preparation for these tests, as well as for tests of facts and ideas, is to be at your physical and mental best. You, no doubt, have your own methods of getting into an exam-taking mood and keeping "in shape." The next section lists some ideas on this subject.

IV. KINDS OF QUESTIONS

Only rarely is the "essay" question, which you answer in narrative form, used in civil service tests. Civil service tests are usually of the short-answer type. Full instructions for answering these questions will be given to you at the examination. But in case this is your first experience with short-answer questions and separate answer sheets, here is what you need to know:

1) Multiple-choice Questions

Most popular of the short-answer questions is the "multiple choice" or "best answer" question. It can be used, for example, to test for factual knowledge, ability to solve problems or judgment in meeting situations found at work.

A multiple-choice question is normally one of three types—
- It can begin with an incomplete statement followed by several possible endings. You are to find the one ending which *best* completes the statement, although some of the others may not be entirely wrong.
- It can also be a complete statement in the form of a question which is answered by choosing one of the statements listed.

- It can be in the form of a problem – again you select the best answer.

Here is an example of a multiple-choice question with a discussion which should give you some clues as to the method for choosing the right answer:

When an employee has a complaint about his assignment, the action which will *best* help him overcome his difficulty is to
A. discuss his difficulty with his coworkers
B. take the problem to the head of the organization
C. take the problem to the person who gave him the assignment
D. say nothing to anyone about his complaint

In answering this question, you should study each of the choices to find which is best. Consider choice "A" – Certainly an employee may discuss his complaint with fellow employees, but no change or improvement can result, and the complaint remains unresolved. Choice "B" is a poor choice since the head of the organization probably does not know what assignment you have been given, and taking your problem to him is known as "going over the head" of the supervisor. The supervisor, or person who made the assignment, is the person who can clarify it or correct any injustice. Choice "C" is, therefore, correct. To say nothing, as in choice "D," is unwise. Supervisors have and interest in knowing the problems employees are facing, and the employee is seeking a solution to his problem.

2) True/False Questions

The "true/false" or "right/wrong" form of question is sometimes used. Here a complete statement is given. Your job is to decide whether the statement is right or wrong.

SAMPLE: A roaming cell-phone call to a nearby city costs less than a non-roaming call to a distant city.

This statement is wrong, or false, since roaming calls are more expensive.

This is not a complete list of all possible question forms, although most of the others are variations of these common types. You will always get complete directions for answering questions. Be sure you understand *how* to mark your answers – ask questions until you do.

V. RECORDING YOUR ANSWERS

Computer terminals are used more and more today for many different kinds of exams.

For an examination with very few applicants, you may be told to record your answers in the test booklet itself. Separate answer sheets are much more common. If this separate answer sheet is to be scored by machine – and this is often the case – it is highly important that you mark your answers correctly in order to get credit.

An electronic scoring machine is often used in civil service offices because of the speed with which papers can be scored. Machine-scored answer sheets must be marked with a pencil, which will be given to you. This pencil has a high graphite content which responds to the electronic scoring machine. As a matter of fact, stray dots may register as answers, so do not let your pencil rest on the answer sheet while you are pondering the correct answer. Also, if your pencil lead breaks or is otherwise defective, ask for another.

Since the answer sheet will be dropped in a slot in the scoring machine, be careful not to bend the corners or get the paper crumpled.

The answer sheet normally has five vertical columns of numbers, with 30 numbers to a column. These numbers correspond to the question numbers in your test booklet. After each number, going across the page are four or five pairs of dotted lines. These short dotted lines have small letters or numbers above them. The first two pairs may also have a "T" or "F" above the letters. This indicates that the first two pairs only are to be used if the questions are of the true-false type. If the questions are multiple choice, disregard the "T" and "F" and pay attention only to the small letters or numbers.

Answer your questions in the manner of the sample that follows:

32. The largest city in the United States is
    A. Washington, D.C.
    B. New York City
    C. Chicago
    D. Detroit
    E. San Francisco

1) Choose the answer you think is best. (New York City is the largest, so "B" is correct.)
2) Find the row of dotted lines numbered the same as the question you are answering. (Find row number 32)
3) Find the pair of dotted lines corresponding to the answer. (Find the pair of lines under the mark "B.")
4) Make a solid black mark between the dotted lines.

VI. BEFORE THE TEST

Common sense will help you find procedures to follow to get ready for an examination. Too many of us, however, overlook these sensible measures. Indeed, nervousness and fatigue have been found to be the most serious reasons why applicants fail to do their best on civil service tests. Here is a list of reminders:

- Begin your preparation early – Don't wait until the last minute to go scurrying around for books and materials or to find out what the position is all about.
- Prepare continuously – An hour a night for a week is better than an all-night cram session. This has been definitely established. What is more, a night a week for a month will return better dividends than crowding your study into a shorter period of time.
- Locate the place of the exam – You have been sent a notice telling you when and where to report for the examination. If the location is in a different town or otherwise unfamiliar to you, it would be well to inquire the best route and learn something about the building.
- Relax the night before the test – Allow your mind to rest. Do not study at all that night. Plan some mild recreation or diversion; then go to bed early and get a good night's sleep.
- Get up early enough to make a leisurely trip to the place for the test – This way unforeseen events, traffic snarls, unfamiliar buildings, etc. will not upset you.
- Dress comfortably – A written test is not a fashion show. You will be known by number and not by name, so wear something comfortable.

- Leave excess paraphernalia at home – Shopping bags and odd bundles will get in your way. You need bring only the items mentioned in the official notice you received; usually everything you need is provided. Do not bring reference books to the exam. They will only confuse those last minutes and be taken away from you when in the test room.
- Arrive somewhat ahead of time – If because of transportation schedules you must get there very early, bring a newspaper or magazine to take your mind off yourself while waiting.
- Locate the examination room – When you have found the proper room, you will be directed to the seat or part of the room where you will sit. Sometimes you are given a sheet of instructions to read while you are waiting. Do not fill out any forms until you are told to do so; just read them and be prepared.
- Relax and prepare to listen to the instructions
- If you have any physical problem that may keep you from doing your best, be sure to tell the test administrator. If you are sick or in poor health, you really cannot do your best on the exam. You can come back and take the test some other time.

VII. AT THE TEST

The day of the test is here and you have the test booklet in your hand. The temptation to get going is very strong. Caution! There is more to success than knowing the right answers. You must know how to identify your papers and understand variations in the type of short-answer question used in this particular examination. Follow these suggestions for maximum results from your efforts:

1) Cooperate with the monitor

The test administrator has a duty to create a situation in which you can be as much at ease as possible. He will give instructions, tell you when to begin, check to see that you are marking your answer sheet correctly, and so on. He is not there to guard you, although he will see that your competitors do not take unfair advantage. He wants to help you do your best.

2) Listen to all instructions

Don't jump the gun! Wait until you understand all directions. In most civil service tests you get more time than you need to answer the questions. So don't be in a hurry. Read each word of instructions until you clearly understand the meaning. Study the examples, listen to all announcements and follow directions. Ask questions if you do not understand what to do.

3) Identify your papers

Civil service exams are usually identified by number only. You will be assigned a number; you must not put your name on your test papers. Be sure to copy your number correctly. Since more than one exam may be given, copy your exact examination title.

4) Plan your time

Unless you are told that a test is a "speed" or "rate of work" test, speed itself is usually not important. Time enough to answer all the questions will be provided, but this does not mean that you have all day. An overall time limit has been set. Divide the total time (in minutes) by the number of questions to determine the approximate time you have for each question.

5) Do not linger over difficult questions

If you come across a difficult question, mark it with a paper clip (useful to have along) and come back to it when you have been through the booklet. One caution if you do this – be sure to skip a number on your answer sheet as well. Check often to be sure that you have not lost your place and that you are marking in the row numbered the same as the question you are answering.

6) Read the questions

Be sure you know what the question asks! Many capable people are unsuccessful because they failed to *read* the questions correctly.

7) Answer all questions

Unless you have been instructed that a penalty will be deducted for incorrect answers, it is better to guess than to omit a question.

8) Speed tests

It is often better NOT to guess on speed tests. It has been found that on timed tests people are tempted to spend the last few seconds before time is called in marking answers at random – without even reading them – in the hope of picking up a few extra points. To discourage this practice, the instructions may warn you that your score will be "corrected" for guessing. That is, a penalty will be applied. The incorrect answers will be deducted from the correct ones, or some other penalty formula will be used.

9) Review your answers

If you finish before time is called, go back to the questions you guessed or omitted to give them further thought. Review other answers if you have time.

10) Return your test materials

If you are ready to leave before others have finished or time is called, take ALL your materials to the monitor and leave quietly. Never take any test material with you. The monitor can discover whose papers are not complete, and taking a test booklet may be grounds for disqualification.

VIII. EXAMINATION TECHNIQUES

1) Read the general instructions carefully. These are usually printed on the first page of the exam booklet. As a rule, these instructions refer to the timing of the examination; the fact that you should not start work until the signal and must stop work at a signal, etc. If there are any *special* instructions, such as a choice of questions to be answered, make sure that you note this instruction carefully.

2) When you are ready to start work on the examination, that is as soon as the signal has been given, read the instructions to each question booklet, underline any key words or phrases, such as *least, best, outline, describe* and the like. In this way you will tend to answer as requested rather than discover on reviewing your paper that you *listed without describing*, that you selected the *worst* choice rather than the *best* choice, etc.

3) If the examination is of the objective or multiple-choice type – that is, each question will also give a series of possible answers: A, B, C or D, and you are called upon to select the best answer and write the letter next to that answer on your answer paper – it is advisable to start answering each question in turn. There may be anywhere from 50 to 100 such questions in the three or four hours allotted and you can see how much time would be taken if you read through all the questions before beginning to answer any. Furthermore, if you come across a question or group of questions which you know would be difficult to answer, it would undoubtedly affect your handling of all the other questions.

4) If the examination is of the essay type and contains but a few questions, it is a moot point as to whether you should read all the questions before starting to answer any one. Of course, if you are given a choice – say five out of seven and the like – then it is essential to read all the questions so you can eliminate the two that are most difficult. If, however, you are asked to answer all the questions, there may be danger in trying to answer the easiest one first because you may find that you will spend too much time on it. The best technique is to answer the first question, then proceed to the second, etc.

5) Time your answers. Before the exam begins, write down the time it started, then add the time allowed for the examination and write down the time it must be completed, then divide the time available somewhat as follows:
   - If 3-1/2 hours are allowed, that would be 210 minutes. If you have 80 objective-type questions, that would be an average of 2-1/2 minutes per question. Allow yourself no more than 2 minutes per question, or a total of 160 minutes, which will permit about 50 minutes to review.
   - If for the time allotment of 210 minutes there are 7 essay questions to answer, that would average about 30 minutes a question. Give yourself only 25 minutes per question so that you have about 35 minutes to review.

6) The most important instruction is to *read each question* and make sure you know what is wanted. The second most important instruction is to *time yourself properly* so that you answer every question. The third most important instruction is to *answer every question*. Guess if you have to but include something for each question. Remember that you will receive no credit for a blank and will probably receive some credit if you write something in answer to an essay question. If you guess a letter – say "B" for a multiple-choice question – you may have guessed right. If you leave a blank as an answer to a multiple-choice question, the examiners may respect your feelings but it will not add a point to your score. Some exams may penalize you for wrong answers, so in such cases *only*, you may not want to guess unless you have some basis for your answer.

7) Suggestions
   a. Objective-type questions
      1. Examine the question booklet for proper sequence of pages and questions
      2. Read all instructions carefully
      3. Skip any question which seems too difficult; return to it after all other questions have been answered
      4. Apportion your time properly; do not spend too much time on any single question or group of questions

5. Note and underline key words – *all, most, fewest, least, best, worst, same, opposite,* etc.
6. Pay particular attention to negatives
7. Note unusual option, e.g., unduly long, short, complex, different or similar in content to the body of the question
8. Observe the use of "hedging" words – *probably, may, most likely,* etc.
9. Make sure that your answer is put next to the same number as the question
10. Do not second-guess unless you have good reason to believe the second answer is definitely more correct
11. Cross out original answer if you decide another answer is more accurate; do not erase until you are ready to hand your paper in
12. Answer all questions; guess unless instructed otherwise
13. Leave time for review

   b. Essay questions
      1. Read each question carefully
      2. Determine exactly what is wanted. Underline key words or phrases.
      3. Decide on outline or paragraph answer
      4. Include many different points and elements unless asked to develop any one or two points or elements
      5. Show impartiality by giving pros and cons unless directed to select one side only
      6. Make and write down any assumptions you find necessary to answer the questions
      7. Watch your English, grammar, punctuation and choice of words
      8. Time your answers; don't crowd material

8) Answering the essay question

Most essay questions can be answered by framing the specific response around several key words or ideas. Here are a few such key words or ideas:

M's: manpower, materials, methods, money, management
P's: purpose, program, policy, plan, procedure, practice, problems, pitfalls, personnel, public relations

   a. Six basic steps in handling problems:
      1. Preliminary plan and background development
      2. Collect information, data and facts
      3. Analyze and interpret information, data and facts
      4. Analyze and develop solutions as well as make recommendations
      5. Prepare report and sell recommendations
      6. Install recommendations and follow up effectiveness

   b. Pitfalls to avoid
      1. *Taking things for granted* – A statement of the situation does not necessarily imply that each of the elements is necessarily true; for example, a complaint may be invalid and biased so that all that can be taken for granted is that a complaint has been registered

2. *Considering only one side of a situation* – Wherever possible, indicate several alternatives and then point out the reasons you selected the best one
3. *Failing to indicate follow up* – Whenever your answer indicates action on your part, make certain that you will take proper follow-up action to see how successful your recommendations, procedures or actions turn out to be
4. *Taking too long in answering any single question* – Remember to time your answers properly

IX. AFTER THE TEST

Scoring procedures differ in detail among civil service jurisdictions although the general principles are the same. Whether the papers are hand-scored or graded by machine we have described, they are nearly always graded by number. That is, the person who marks the paper knows only the number – never the name – of the applicant. Not until all the papers have been graded will they be matched with names. If other tests, such as training and experience or oral interview ratings have been given, scores will be combined. Different parts of the examination usually have different weights. For example, the written test might count 60 percent of the final grade, and a rating of training and experience 40 percent. In many jurisdictions, veterans will have a certain number of points added to their grades.

After the final grade has been determined, the names are placed in grade order and an eligible list is established. There are various methods for resolving ties between those who get the same final grade – probably the most common is to place first the name of the person whose application was received first. Job offers are made from the eligible list in the order the names appear on it. You will be notified of your grade and your rank as soon as all these computations have been made. This will be done as rapidly as possible.

People who are found to meet the requirements in the announcement are called "eligibles." Their names are put on a list of eligible candidates. An eligible's chances of getting a job depend on how high he stands on this list and how fast agencies are filling jobs from the list.

When a job is to be filled from a list of eligibles, the agency asks for the names of people on the list of eligibles for that job. When the civil service commission receives this request, it sends to the agency the names of the three people highest on this list. Or, if the job to be filled has specialized requirements, the office sends the agency the names of the top three persons who meet these requirements from the general list.

The appointing officer makes a choice from among the three people whose names were sent to him. If the selected person accepts the appointment, the names of the others are put back on the list to be considered for future openings.

That is the rule in hiring from all kinds of eligible lists, whether they are for typist, carpenter, chemist, or something else. For every vacancy, the appointing officer has his choice of any one of the top three eligibles on the list. This explains why the person whose name is on top of the list sometimes does not get an appointment when some of the persons lower on the list do. If the appointing officer chooses the second or third eligible, the No. 1 eligible does not get a job at once, but stays on the list until he is appointed or the list is terminated.

X. HOW TO PASS THE INTERVIEW TEST

The examination for which you applied requires an oral interview test. You have already taken the written test and you are now being called for the interview test – the final part of the formal examination.

You may think that it is not possible to prepare for an interview test and that there are no procedures to follow during an interview. Our purpose is to point out some things you can do in advance that will help you and some good rules to follow and pitfalls to avoid while you are being interviewed.

What is an interview supposed to test?

The written examination is designed to test the technical knowledge and competence of the candidate; the oral is designed to evaluate intangible qualities, not readily measured otherwise, and to establish a list showing the relative fitness of each candidate – as measured against his competitors – for the position sought. Scoring is not on the basis of "right" and "wrong," but on a sliding scale of values ranging from "not passable" to "outstanding." As a matter of fact, it is possible to achieve a relatively low score without a single "incorrect" answer because of evident weakness in the qualities being measured.

Occasionally, an examination may consist entirely of an oral test – either an individual or a group oral. In such cases, information is sought concerning the technical knowledges and abilities of the candidate, since there has been no written examination for this purpose. More commonly, however, an oral test is used to supplement a written examination.

Who conducts interviews?

The composition of oral boards varies among different jurisdictions. In nearly all, a representative of the personnel department serves as chairman. One of the members of the board may be a representative of the department in which the candidate would work. In some cases, "outside experts" are used, and, frequently, a businessman or some other representative of the general public is asked to serve. Labor and management or other special groups may be represented. The aim is to secure the services of experts in the appropriate field.

However the board is composed, it is a good idea (and not at all improper or unethical) to ascertain in advance of the interview who the members are and what groups they represent. When you are introduced to them, you will have some idea of their backgrounds and interests, and at least you will not stutter and stammer over their names.

What should be done before the interview?

While knowledge about the board members is useful and takes some of the surprise element out of the interview, there is other preparation which is more substantive. It *is* possible to prepare for an oral interview – in several ways:

1) Keep a copy of your application and review it carefully before the interview

This may be the only document before the oral board, and the starting point of the interview. Know what education and experience you have listed there, and the sequence and dates of all of it. Sometimes the board will ask you to review the highlights of your experience for them; you should not have to hem and haw doing it.

2) Study the class specification and the examination announcement

Usually, the oral board has one or both of these to guide them. The qualities, characteristics or knowledges required by the position sought are stated in these documents. They offer valuable clues as to the nature of the oral interview. For example, if the job involves supervisory responsibilities, the announcement will usually indicate that knowledge of modern supervisory methods and the qualifications of the candidate as a supervisor will be tested. If so, you can expect such questions, frequently in the form of a hypothetical situation which you are expected to solve. NEVER go into an oral without knowledge of the duties and responsibilities of the job you seek.

3) Think through each qualification required

Try to visualize the kind of questions you would ask if you were a board member. How well could you answer them? Try especially to appraise your own knowledge and background in each area, *measured against the job sought*, and identify any areas in which you are weak. Be critical and realistic – do not flatter yourself.

4) Do some general reading in areas in which you feel you may be weak

For example, if the job involves supervision and your past experience has NOT, some general reading in supervisory methods and practices, particularly in the field of human relations, might be useful. Do NOT study agency procedures or detailed manuals. The oral board will be testing your understanding and capacity, not your memory.

5) Get a good night's sleep and watch your general health and mental attitude

You will want a clear head at the interview. Take care of a cold or any other minor ailment, and of course, no hangovers.

What should be done on the day of the interview?

Now comes the day of the interview itself. Give yourself plenty of time to get there. Plan to arrive somewhat ahead of the scheduled time, particularly if your appointment is in the fore part of the day. If a previous candidate fails to appear, the board might be ready for you a bit early. By early afternoon an oral board is almost invariably behind schedule if there are many candidates, and you may have to wait. Take along a book or magazine to read, or your application to review, but leave any extraneous material in the waiting room when you go in for your interview. In any event, relax and compose yourself.

The matter of dress is important. The board is forming impressions about you – from your experience, your manners, your attitude, and your appearance. Give your personal appearance careful attention. Dress your best, but not your flashiest. Choose conservative, appropriate clothing, and be sure it is immaculate. This is a business interview, and your appearance should indicate that you regard it as such. Besides, being well groomed and properly dressed will help boost your confidence.

Sooner or later, someone will call your name and escort you into the interview room. *This is it.* From here on you are on your own. It is too late for any more preparation. But remember, you asked for this opportunity to prove your fitness, and you are here because your request was granted.

What happens when you go in?

The usual sequence of events will be as follows: The clerk (who is often the board stenographer) will introduce you to the chairman of the oral board, who will introduce you to the other members of the board. Acknowledge the introductions before you sit down. Do not be surprised if you find a microphone facing you or a stenotypist sitting by. Oral interviews are usually recorded in the event of an appeal or other review.

Usually the chairman of the board will open the interview by reviewing the highlights of your education and work experience from your application – primarily for the benefit of the other members of the board, as well as to get the material into the record. Do not interrupt or comment unless there is an error or significant misinterpretation; if that is the case, do not hesitate. But do not quibble about insignificant matters. Also, he will usually ask you some question about your education, experience or your present job – partly to get you to start talking and to establish the interviewing "rapport." He may start the actual questioning, or turn it over to one of the other members. Frequently, each member undertakes the questioning on a particular area, one in which he is perhaps most competent, so you can expect each member to participate in the examination. Because time is limited, you may also expect some rather abrupt switches in the direction the questioning takes, so do not be upset by it. Normally, a board member will not pursue a single line of questioning unless he discovers a particular strength or weakness.

After each member has participated, the chairman will usually ask whether any member has any further questions, then will ask you if you have anything you wish to add. Unless you are expecting this question, it may floor you. Worse, it may start you off on an extended, extemporaneous speech. The board is not usually seeking more information. The question is principally to offer you a last opportunity to present further qualifications or to indicate that you have nothing to add. So, if you feel that a significant qualification or characteristic has been overlooked, it is proper to point it out in a sentence or so. Do not compliment the board on the thoroughness of their examination – they have been sketchy, and you know it. If you wish, merely say, "No thank you, I have nothing further to add." This is a point where you can "talk yourself out" of a good impression or fail to present an important bit of information. Remember, *you close the interview yourself*.

The chairman will then say, "That is all, Mr. _____, thank you." Do not be startled; the interview is over, and quicker than you think. Thank him, gather your belongings and take your leave. Save your sigh of relief for the other side of the door.

How to put your best foot forward

Throughout this entire process, you may feel that the board individually and collectively is trying to pierce your defenses, seek out your hidden weaknesses and embarrass and confuse you. Actually, this is not true. They are obliged to make an appraisal of your qualifications for the job you are seeking, and they want to see you in your best light. Remember, they must interview all candidates and a non-cooperative candidate may become a failure in spite of their best efforts to bring out his qualifications. Here are 15 suggestions that will help you:

1) Be natural – Keep your attitude confident, not cocky

If you are not confident that you can do the job, do not expect the board to be. Do not apologize for your weaknesses, try to bring out your strong points. The board is interested in a positive, not negative, presentation. Cockiness will antagonize any board member and make him wonder if you are covering up a weakness by a false show of strength.

2) Get comfortable, but don't lounge or sprawl

Sit erectly but not stiffly. A careless posture may lead the board to conclude that you are careless in other things, or at least that you are not impressed by the importance of the occasion. Either conclusion is natural, even if incorrect. Do not fuss with your clothing, a pencil or an ashtray. Your hands may occasionally be useful to emphasize a point; do not let them become a point of distraction.

3) Do not wisecrack or make small talk

This is a serious situation, and your attitude should show that you consider it as such. Further, the time of the board is limited – they do not want to waste it, and neither should you.

4) Do not exaggerate your experience or abilities

In the first place, from information in the application or other interviews and sources, the board may know more about you than you think. Secondly, you probably will not get away with it. An experienced board is rather adept at spotting such a situation, so do not take the chance.

5) If you know a board member, do not make a point of it, yet do not hide it

Certainly you are not fooling him, and probably not the other members of the board. Do not try to take advantage of your acquaintanceship – it will probably do you little good.

6) Do not dominate the interview

Let the board do that. They will give you the clues – do not assume that you have to do all the talking. Realize that the board has a number of questions to ask you, and do not try to take up all the interview time by showing off your extensive knowledge of the answer to the first one.

7) Be attentive

You only have 20 minutes or so, and you should keep your attention at its sharpest throughout. When a member is addressing a problem or question to you, give him your undivided attention. Address your reply principally to him, but do not exclude the other board members.

8) Do not interrupt

A board member may be stating a problem for you to analyze. He will ask you a question when the time comes. Let him state the problem, and wait for the question.

9) Make sure you understand the question

Do not try to answer until you are sure what the question is. If it is not clear, restate it in your own words or ask the board member to clarify it for you. However, do not haggle about minor elements.

10) Reply promptly but not hastily

A common entry on oral board rating sheets is "candidate responded readily," or "candidate hesitated in replies." Respond as promptly and quickly as you can, but do not jump to a hasty, ill-considered answer.

11) Do not be peremptory in your answers

A brief answer is proper – but do not fire your answer back. That is a losing game from your point of view. The board member can probably ask questions much faster than you can answer them.

12) Do not try to create the answer you think the board member wants

He is interested in what kind of mind you have and how it works – not in playing games. Furthermore, he can usually spot this practice and will actually grade you down on it.

13) Do not switch sides in your reply merely to agree with a board member

Frequently, a member will take a contrary position merely to draw you out and to see if you are willing and able to defend your point of view. Do not start a debate, yet do not surrender a good position. If a position is worth taking, it is worth defending.

14) Do not be afraid to admit an error in judgment if you are shown to be wrong

The board knows that you are forced to reply without any opportunity for careful consideration. Your answer may be demonstrably wrong. If so, admit it and get on with the interview.

15) Do not dwell at length on your present job

The opening question may relate to your present assignment. Answer the question but do not go into an extended discussion. You are being examined for a *new* job, not your present one. As a matter of fact, try to phrase ALL your answers in terms of the job for which you are being examined.

Basis of Rating

Probably you will forget most of these "do's" and "don'ts" when you walk into the oral interview room. Even remembering them all will not ensure you a passing grade. Perhaps you did not have the qualifications in the first place. But remembering them will help you to put your best foot forward, without treading on the toes of the board members.

Rumor and popular opinion to the contrary notwithstanding, an oral board wants you to make the best appearance possible. They know you are under pressure – but they also want to see how you respond to it as a guide to what your reaction would be under the pressures of the job you seek. They will be influenced by the degree of poise you display, the personal traits you show and the manner in which you respond.

ABOUT THIS BOOK

This book contains tests divided into Examination Sections. Go through each test, answering every question in the margin. We have also attached a sample answer sheet at the back of the book that can be removed and used. At the end of each test look at the answer key and check your answers. On the ones you got wrong, look at the right answer choice and learn. Do not fill in the answers first. Do not memorize the questions and answers, but understand the answer and principles involved. On your test, the questions will likely be different from the samples. Questions are changed and new ones added. If you understand these past questions you should have success with any changes that arise. Tests may consist of several types of questions. We have additional books on each subject should more study be advisable or necessary for you. Finally, the more you study, the better prepared you will be. This book is intended to be the last thing you study before you walk into the examination room. Prior study of relevant texts is also recommended. NLC publishes some of these in our Fundamental Series. Knowledge and good sense are important factors in passing your exam. Good luck also helps. So now study this Passbook, absorb the material contained within and take that knowledge into the examination. Then do your best to pass that exam.

EXAMINATION SECTION

EXAMINATION SECTION
TEST 1

DIRECTIONS: Each question or incomplete statement is followed by several suggested answers or completions. Select the one that BEST answers the question or completes the statement. *PRINT THE LETTER OF THE CORRECT ANSWER IN THE SPACE AT THE RIGHT.*

1. When filling an empty aqueduct, the valve should be opened 1.____

    A. slowly to prevent damage to the aqueduct
    B. rapidly to fill the line as soon as possible
    C. slowly to prevent rapid lowering of the reservoir level
    D. rapidly so that there are no air locks

2. The BEST way of detecting the location of a suspected chlorine leak is by placing a _____ near the suspected leak. 2.____

    A. rag, which has been dipped in a strong ammonia water,
    B. match
    C. piece of litmus paper
    D. flow meter

3. The term *run-off* refers to the 3.____

    A. amount a valve must be turned in order to open it fully
    B. length of time an electric motor continues to turn after the current is shut off
    C. amount of rainfall which flows from the ground surface into the streams and reservoirs
    D. distance the water falls from the intake gate to the turbine

4. Algae in reservoirs may be killed by using 4.____

    A. zeolite   B. copper sulphate
    C. sodium chloride   D. calcium chloride

5. The one of the following types of valves that USUALLY operates without manual control is a(n) _____ valve. 5.____

    A. check   B. globe   C. gate   D. angle

6. Rate of flow of water through a water treatment plant is USUALLY referred to in terms of 6.____

    A. c.f.s.   B. c.f.m.   C. r.p.m.   D. m.g.d.

7. In order to make it easier to operate a large valve or gate, pressures on both sides of the valve or gate are balanced by 7.____

    A. using weights on each side of the valve or gate
    B. opening a smaller by-pass valve
    C. partially shutting down the water in the upstream line
    D. opening the downstream valve very slowly

8. Leaves are removed from the water entering the treatment plant or aqueduct by 8.____

    A. skimming   B. coagulating   C. draining   D. screening

9. Odors, due to gases in the water, are removed by

   A. surging   B. sluicing   C. aerating   D. clarifying

10. Chlorine residual refers to the

    A. amount of chlorine that must be added to the water
    B. amount of chlorine that remains in the water after a given period
    C. method of adding the chlorine to the water
    D. method of protecting personnel using chlorine from the effects of the chlorine

11. One of the processes that takes place in an Imhoff tank is

    A. oxidation   B. flocculation   C. digestion   D. coagulation

12. As used in a sewage disposal plant, *effluent* refers to the

    A. basic treatment process of sewage
    B. time it takes for complete treatment of sewage
    C. type of control the plant uses for treatment
    D. final liquid coming out of the treatment process

13. A grit chamber operates on the basis that

    A. grit will settle out of slow-moving water
    B. grit will float and can be removed by skimming the surface
    C. increasing the rate of flow of water will leave the grit behind
    D. spraying water into the air will cause the heavier grit to separate from the water

14. The purpose of sedimentation in any sewage treatment process is to

    A. aerate the sewage
    B. increase the chlorine content of the sewage
    C. remove suspended matter from the sewage
    D. kill the bacteria in the sewage

15. The final treatment for sludge before it is disposed of is

    A. drying   B. adding chlorine
    C. mixing   D. washing

16. The amount of sewage applied to a filter bed is GENERALLY controlled by a

    A. sluice gate   B. flow meter
    C. dosing siphon   D. regulating valve

17. Methane gas which results from the sewage treatment process is MOST frequently

    A. vented to the outside air to prevent injury to plant personnel
    B. used as a fuel in the plant
    C. combined with other gases to render it harmless
    D. burned in the open air

18. The filtering material in a *filter bed* at a sewage treatment plant is USUALLY

    A. activated charcoal   B. sand
    C. alum   D. ammonium chloride

19. Cleaning sewer lines is USUALLY done by the use of a   19.____

    A. catch basin   B. flushometer
    C. sewer rod   D. center line

20. One of the ways of locating a leak in a water line is by using a   20.____

    A. manometer   B. sounding rod
    C. poling board   D. diffusor

21. MOST sewer pipes are made of   21.____

    A. cast iron   B. agricultural tile
    C. brass   D. copper

22. One of the materials generally used in caulking joints in bell and spigot pipe is   22.____

    A. tar   B. litharge   C. red lead   D. oakum

23. Water pipe must be laid at least two feet below the ground surface MAINLY to   23.____

    A. prevent freezing
    B. discourage malicious tampering
    C. reduce the pressure required to make the water flow
    D. eliminate possibility of damage to roads in case of water main break

24. When soldering copper gutters, the flux that is GENERALLY used is   24.____

    A. sal ammoniac   B. resin
    C. killed muriatic acid   D. calcium chloride

25. A good concrete mix for use in the foundations of a small building is   25.____

    A. 1:2:5   B. 5:2:1   C. 2:5:1   D. 1:5:2

26. When painting steel, red lead is used MAINLY as a   26.____

    A. primer coat so final coat will adhere better
    B. primer coat to protect the steel from rusting
    C. finish coat to protect the steel from the action of the sun and water
    D. second coat to bind the primer and finish coats

27. Studs in frame buildings are USUALLY   27.____

    A. 1" x 4"   B. 1" x 6"   C. 2" x 4"   D. 2" x 6"

28. A cement mortar used in brickwork is USUALLY made more workable by adding   28.____

    A. phosphate   B. lime   C. calcium   D. grout

Questions 29-32.

DIRECTIONS: The following four questions numbered 29 to 32, inclusive, are to be answered in accordance with the rules of the department of water supply, gas and electricity.

29. The term *water course* refers to

    A. aqueducts only
    B. pipe lines only
    C. natural or artificial streams only
    D. all of the above

30. Where a swimming pool discharges upon or into the ground and the water is not treated, the minimum distance between such discharge and a stream MUST be at least _____ feet.

    A. 50   B. 100   C. 250   D. 450

31. According to the above rules, clothes may

    A. be washed in a spring, if the spring does not feed directly into a reservoir
    B. be washed in a spring if the place where this is being done is at least one mile from a reservoir
    C. be washed in a spring provided a chlorinated soap is used
    D. not be washed in a spring

32. Industrial wastes may

    A. be discharged into a stream provided the stream does not feed directly into a reservoir
    B. be discharged into a stream, provided the point of discharge is at least one mile from a reservoir
    C. be discharged into a stream if the wastes are purified in an approved manner
    D. not be discharged into a stream

33. One method of determining the height of the water in a stream feeding into a reservoir is by means of a

    A. venturi meter   B. flow meter
    C. hook gage   D. strain gage

34. When digging a deep trench, the sides are USUALLY prevented from caving in by using

    A. shoulders   B. blocking   C. pins   D. sheathing

35. The FIRST precaution a worker should take before entering a sewer manhole is to

    A. put on hard-toed shoes
    B. put on safety goggles
    C. check that the next manhole upstream is not obstructed
    D. test the air in the manhole

36. Assume that a fuse blows upon connecting a light load to the circuit. You replace it with the same size fuse, and again the fuse blows.
    The BEST thing to do in this case is to

    A. connect a wire across the fuse so it cannot blow under such a light load
    B. replace the fuse with one having a higher rating
    C. check the wiring of the circuit
    D. place two fuses in series to prevent blowing

37. Of the following material, the one that is BEST for fill as a subgrade for a road is 37._____

    A. sand
    B. silt
    C. clay
    D. a mixture of sand, silt, and clay

38. When dealing with leaking chlorine, it is IMPORTANT to remember that chlorine is 38._____

    A. highly flammable
    B. made safe by spraying water on it
    C. not corrosive
    D. heavier than air

39. Cast iron pipe is MOST frequently cut with a(n) 39._____

    A. hack saw
    B. diamond point chisel
    C. burning torch
    D. abrasive wheel

40. Water hammer in a pipe line is BEST reduced by installing 40._____

    A. a pressure regulator
    B. an air chamber
    C. smaller pipes and valves
    D. larger pipes and valves

KEY (CORRECT ANSWERS)

1. A	11. C	21. A	31. D
2. A	12. D	22. D	32. D
3. C	13. A	23. A	33. C
4. B	14. C	24. C	34. D
5. A	15. A	25. A	35. D
6. D	16. C	26. B	36. C
7. B	17. B	27. C	37. D
8. D	18. B	28. B	38. D
9. C	19. C	29. D	39. B
10. B	20. B	30. B	40. B

TEST 2

DIRECTIONS: Each question or incomplete statement is followed by several suggested answers or completions. Select the one that BEST answers the question or completes the statement. *PRINT THE LETTER OF THE CORRECT ANSWER IN SPACE AT THE RIGHT.*

1. When used in conjunction with a centrifugal pump, a foot valve 1.____

    A. equalizes the pressure on both sides of the pump
    B. regulates the amount of water flowing through the pump
    C. prevents water in the pump from flowing back down the suction line
    D. adjusts the speed of the pump to the amount of water to be pumped

2. Grounding an electric motor is 2.____

    A. *good* practice because the motor will operate better
    B. *poor* practice because the motor will not operate as well
    C. *good* practice because it protects against shock hazards
    D. *poor* practice because it increases shock hazards

3. The one of the following wrenches that should NOT be used to turn a nut is a wrench. 3.____

    A. monkey   B. box   C. stillson   D. socket

4. A drill is GENERALLY removed from the chuck of a portable electric drill by using a 4.____

    A. drift pin   B. wedge
    C. centerpunch   D. key

5. The finished surface of a dirt road is MOST frequently maintained with a 5.____

    A. blade grader   B. bulldozer
    C. dragline   D. carryall

6. Frequent stalling of a truck engine is MOST probably due to a 6.____

    A. weak battery   B. low battery water level
    C. leaking oil filter   D. dirty carburetor

7. If the reading of the oil pressure gage on a gasoline motor should suddenly drop to zero, the FIRST thing the operator should do is to 7.____

    A. check the filter
    B. inspect the oil lines
    C. tighten the oil pan bolts
    D. stop the motor

8. A tractor is to be stored for two months. In order to keep it in BEST condition, it should be 8.____

    A. drained of all fuel and oil
    B. lubricated every week
    C. started up periodically and run until warm
    D. steam cleaned and all water drained from the radiator

9. Trees suffering from transplanting shock are quickly helped by 9.____

  A. deep watering   B. foliage feeding
  C. root feeding   D. vitamin treatments

10. For MOST rapid healing, trees should be pruned during   10.____

  A. November, December, and January
  B. February, March, and April
  C. May, June, and July
  D. August, September, and October

11. The blades of a lawn mower should be set so that the blades   11.____

  A. firmly touch the bed knife
  B. barely touch the bed knife
  C. clear the bed knife by 1/16 inch
  D. clear the bed knife by 1/8 inch

12. The MAIN reason for mulching is to   12.____

  A. fertilize the soil
  B. prevent erosion
  C. protect plants from the cold
  D. kill insects

13. A compost heap would MOST likely include   13.____

  A. lawn clippings   B. sand
  C. stumps of trees   D. gravel

14. Of the following statements with regard to *seeding,* the one that is CORRECT is: 14.____

  A. Seeds should be sown on a windy day
  B. The ground should be watered heavily after seeding
  C. Seeding should be done primarily on a bright and sunny day
  D. It is not necessary to carefully apportion the amount of seeds sown

15. Organic matter is often added to soil to better condition it for growing plants.   15.____
Of the following, the item that is NOT organic matter is

  A. lime   B. peat   C. manure   D. leaf mold

16. Of the following, the BEST way to store coniferous seedlings which cannot be planted   16.____
for a few days is to

  A. unwrap them and put them in a dark, dry location
  B. place them flat on the ground in a sunny location so they can get plenty of light and air
  C. place them in a trench dug in the earth and cover the root ends with soil
  D. make sure the ball is not loosened and keep in a hothouse

17. Transplanting of seedlings is BEST done in early   17.____

  A. spring   B. summer   C. autumn   D. winter

18. After planting privet hedges, they are frequently cut back to within a few inches of the ground.
    This is USUALLY done to

    A. remove dead parts of the hedge
    B. insure dense growth from the ground up
    C. speed up root development
    D. reduce the possibility of insect damage while the hedge is taking root

18.____

19. *Heaving* of pavements in wintertime is USUALLY caused by the

    A. difference of expansion of pavement and subgrade
    B. freezing of water in subgrade
    C. loss of bond between pavement and subgrade
    D. brittleness of pavement

19.____

20. Erosion of side slopes caused by the action of water is GREATEST when the soil is

    A. silt   B. clay   C. hardpan   D. silty-clay

20.____

21. The MAIN reason for making a crown in a road pavement is to

    A. reduce the amount of paving material necessary
    B. make it easier for cars to go around a curve
    C. drain surface water
    D. increase the strength of the pavement where it is most needed

21.____

22. The MAIN reason for paving ditches at the side of a road is to

    A. prevent damage from cars
    B. permit the ditch to carry more water
    C. prevent erosion of the soil in the ditch
    D. block water from getting under the pavement

22.____

23. Assume that vitrified clay tile pipe, with open joints, is being used as the underdrain for a roadway.
    This pipe should be laid

    A. directly on the bottom of the trench
    B. on a bed of clay
    C. on a bed of peat
    D. on a bed of gravel

23.____

24. A macadam road is one in which the base is GENERALLY made of

    A. asphalt   B. broken stone
    C. concrete   D. stabilized soil

24.____

25. To loosen compacted rocky earth road surfaces, the BEST piece of equipment to use is a

    A. disc harrow   B. drag line   C. bulldozer   D. scarifier

25.____

26. Oiling of an earth road is BEST done

    A. in the winter before the snow falls
    B. when you expect much rain

26.____

C. in the spring during dry weather
D. immediately after snow is cleared from the road

27. Cracks in concrete roads are BEST repaired by filling them with

   A. tar
   B. grout
   C. mineral filler
   D. sand

27._____

28. When repairing patches in old asphalt pavements, the edges of the patch should FIRST be painted with

   A. the same material used for the patch
   B. kerosene
   C. asphalt cement
   D. asphalt binder

28._____

29. The sum of 3 1/4, 5 1/8, 2 1/2, and 3 3/8 is

   A. 14   B. 14 1/8   C. 14 1/4   D. 14 3/8

29._____

30. Assume that it takes 6 men 8 days to do a particular job.
   If you have only 4 men available to do this job and they all work at the same speed, then the number of days it would take to complete the job would be

   A. 11   B. 12   C. 13   D. 14

30._____

31. The city aims to supply *potable* water. As used in this sentence, the word *potable* means MOST NEARLY

   A. clear   B. drinkable   C. fresh   D. adequate

31._____

32. Water, after being purified, should not be turbid. As used in this sentence, the word turbid means MOST NEARLY

   A. cloudy   B. warm   C. infected   D. hard

32._____

33. The flow of water is *impeded* by the silt in the bottom of the stream.
   As used in this sentence, the word *impeded* means MOST NEARLY

   A. dammed   B. hindered   C. helped   D. dirtied

33._____

Questions 34-35.

DIRECTIONS: Questions 34 and 35 are based on the following paragraph.

Repeated burning of the same area should be avoided. Burning should not be done on impervious, shallow, unstable, or highly erodible soils, or on steep slopes - especially in areas subject to heavy rains or rapid snowmelt. When existing vegetation is likely to be killed or seriously weakened by the fire, measures should be taken to assure prompt revegetation of the burned area. Burns should be limited to relatively small proportions of a watershed unit so that the stream channels will be able to carry any increased flows with a minimum of damage.

34. According to the above paragraph, planned burning should be limited to small areas of the watershed because

    A. the fire can be better controlled
    B. existing vegetation will be less likely to be killed
    C. plants will grow quicker in small areas
    D. there will be less likelihood of damaging floods

35. According to the above paragraph, burning usually should be done on soils that

    A. readily absorb moisture
    B. have been burnt before
    C. exist as a thin layer over rock
    D. can be flooded by nearby streams

36. If a foreman does not understand the instructions that are given to him by the district engineer, the BEST thing to do is to

    A. work out the solution to the problem himself
    B. do the job in the way he thinks is best
    C. get one of the other foremen to do the job
    D. ask that the instructions be repeated and clarified

37. The BEST foreman is the one who

    A. can work as fast as the fastest man in the crew
    B. is the most skilled mechanic
    C. can get the most work out of the men
    D. is the strongest man

38. Complimenting a man for good work is

    A. *good* practice since it will give the man an incentive to continue working well
    B. *poor* practice because the other men will become jealous
    C. *good* practice because in the future the foreman will not have to supervise this man
    D. *poor* practice since the man should work well without needing compliments

39. In dealing with his men, it is MOST important that a foreman be

    A. a disciplinarian   B. stern
    C. fair   D. chummy with his men

40. When issuing a violation to a member of the public, it is MOST important that a foreman be

    A. aloof and refuse to discuss the violation
    B. stern, and warn the person to correct the violation immediately
    C. courteous and explain what must be done to correct the violation
    D. friendly and volunteer assistance to correct the violation

KEY (CORRECT ANSWERS)

1. C	11. B	21. C	31. B
2. C	12. C	22. C	32. A
3. C	13. A	23. D	33. B
4. D	14. B	24. B	34. D
5. A	15. A	25. D	35. A
6. D	16. C	26. C	36. D
7. D	17. A	27. A	37. C
8. C	18. B	28. C	38. A
9. B	19. B	29. C	39. C
10. B	20. A	30. B	40. C

EXAMINATION SECTION
TEST 1

DIRECTIONS: Each question or incomplete statement is followed by several suggested answers or completions. Select the one that BEST answers the question or completes the statement. *PRINT THE LETTER OF THE CORRECT ANSWER IN THE SPACE AT THE RIGHT.*

Questions 1-5.

DIRECTIONS: Questions 1 through 5, inclusive, refer to the distribution map shown on the LAST page of this test. All questions are to be answered in accordance with this map.

1. The symbol just west of the boundary gate symbol on 21st Street between Willow Avenue and Meadow Avenue is a

    A. hydrant
    B. gate valve
    C. check valve
    D. reducer

2. The number of hydrants on the 30" main in Meadow Avenue between 22nd Street and 23rd Street is

    A. none   B. 1   C. 2   D. 3

3. The S symbol on the main at the west end of 18th Street means that the main is

    A. a special casting
    B. made of steel
    C. shut down
    D. high pressure service

4. A cap is located at or near the intersection of _____ Street and _____ Avenue.

    A. 24th; Willow
    B. 22nd; Willow
    C. 26th; Meadow
    D. 21st; Central

5. A blow off is located in

    A. Meadow Avenue between 19th & 20th Streets
    B. 22nd Street between Willow Avenue and Meadow Avenue
    C. Wilen Avenue between 22nd and 23rd Streets
    D. 22nd Street between Willow Avenue and Central Avenue

6. Assume that a normally sober man appears on the job intoxicated.
Of the following, the BEST procedure for a foreman to follow is to

    A. give the man an easy job so that he cannot get hurt
    B. let the man *sleep it off* in the morning and put him to work in the afternoon
    C. let the man work at his normal duties but keep an *eye* on him
    D. send him home for the day

7. The Chief Engineer has decided to change the procedure that must be followed in making certain types of repairs. The one of the following statements concerning the new procedure that is CORRECT is:
The men

A. should know why the procedure is being changed because they will then be more interested in the job
B. do not have to know the reason for the change because they need do only the work as they are told
C. should know why the procedure is being changed so that they can decide which method of doing the job is better
D. do not have to know the reason for the change because they are not capable of judging the best method of doing a job

8. A foreman, by mistake, orders his men to do a job improperly.
Of the following, the BEST thing for the foreman to do when he realizes his error is to

    A. insist that the job be done as he ordered so that his mistake will not be discovered
    B. admit that he made the mistake and correct the order
    C. tell the men that the order came from *higher up so* that he will not be blamed for the mistake
    D. tell the men that he is merely trying this out to see if it works better

8____

9. The BEST foreman is usually the

    A. fastest worker
    B. man who is most familiar with the streets in the borough
    C. strongest man
    D. man who is most tactful

9____

10. A good foreman will

    A. look after the welfare of his men
    B. demand perfection in the work of his men at all times
    C. make special efforts to impress his superiors
    D. cover up for the actions of his men

10____

11. As a newly appointed foreman, it is MOST important that you

    A. show the men who is boss by issuing orders
    B. prove to the men that you know more than they do
    C. become acquainted with the men and their abilities
    D. show the men how friendly you are

11____

12. A foreman who criticizes his department head is a

    A. *good* foreman, because the men will feel he is on their side
    B. *poor* foreman, because the men will lose respect for him
    C. *good* foreman, because he will get more work done
    D. *poor* foreman, because he will have no time to do his own work

12____

13. One of the men in your gang comes to you, the foreman, and complains that the men in the gang have taken a dislike to him and are making trouble for him.
Of the following, the BEST thing for you to do is to

    A. tell the man he must learn to get along with the other men
    B. report the matter to your superior
    C. call the gang together and tell them they must stop making trouble
    D. investigate the complaint to determine what the problem is

13____

14. As a foreman, you are inspecting the damage done by water from a broken main leaking into the basement of a store. After inspecting the damage, the owner complains to you about the conduct of the men who made the repair.
    Of the following, the BEST way of handling this situation is to tell the owner that

    A. you are there to inspect the damage to the premises only
    B. he should make his complaint to higher authorities
    C. his complaint will be investigated and, if found correct, proper action will be taken
    D. nothing can be done at this time since the men are no longer at this location

Questions 15-17.

DIRECTIONS: Questions 15 through 17, inclusive, are based on the paragraph below. These questions are to be answered in accordance with the information given in this paragraph.

Excavation of trench. The trench shall be excavated as directed; one side of the street or avenue shall be left open for traffic at all times. In paved streets, the length of trench that may be opened between the point where the backfilling has been completed and the point where the pavement is being removed shall not exceed fifteen hundred feet for pipes 24 inches or less in diameter. For pipes larger than 24 inch, the length of open trenches shall not exceed one thousand feet. The completion of the backfilling shall be interpreted to mean the backfilling of the trench and the consolidation of the backfill so that vehicular traffic can be resumed over the backfill, and also the placing of any temporary pavement that *may* be required.

15. According to the above paragraph, the street

    A. can be closed to traffic in emergencies
    B. can be closed to traffic only when laying more than 1500 feet of pipe
    C. is closed to traffic as directed
    D. shall be left open for traffic at all times

16. According to the above paragraph, the MAXIMUM length of open trench permitted in paved streets depends on the

    A. traffic on the street
    B. type of ground that is being excaVated
    C. water conditions met with in excavation
    D. diameter of the pipe being laid

17. According to the above paragraph, the one of the following items that is included in the *completion of the back-filling* is

    A. sheeting and bracing   B. cradle
    C. temporary pavement   D. bridging

Questions 18-20.

DIRECTIONS: Questions 18 through 20, inclusive, are based on the paragraph below. These questions are to be answered in accordance with the information given in this paragraph.

The Contractor shall notify the Engineer by noon of the day immediately preceding the date when he wishes to shut down any main, and if the time set be approved, the Contractor shall provide the men necessary to shut down the main at the time stipulated, and to previously notify all consumers whose supply may be affected. These men shall be under the direction of the Department employees, who will superintend all operations of valves and hydrants. Shutdowns for making connections will not be made unless and until the Contractor has everything on the ground in readiness for the work.

18. According to the above paragraph, before a contractor can make a shut-down, he MUST notify the

    A. Police Department
    B. district foreman
    C. engineer
    D. highway department

19. According to the above paragraph, the operation of the valves will be supervised by the

    A. department employees
    B. contractor's men
    C. contractor's superintendent
    D. engineer

20. According to the above paragraph, shut-downs for connections are made

    A. the day before the connection is made
    B. first and then consumers are notified
    C. at any time convenient to the contractor
    D. when the contractor has everything on the ground in readiness for the work

21. Water hammer in a pipe line is MOST frequently caused by _____ a valve too _____.

    A. opening; rapidly
    B. opening; slowly
    C. closing; rapidly
    D. closing; slowly

22. In using a hacksaw, pressure should be applied to the hacksaw when

    A. pushing it
    B. pulling it
    C. pushing and pulling it
    D. either pushing or pulling, depending upon the way the cut is to be made

23. When cutting cast iron (other than pipe) with a hacksaw, the PROPER number of teeth per inch in the blade should be

    A. 14   B. 18   C. 24   D. 32

24. Concrete is a mixture of cement and

    A. lime, sand, and water
    B. sand and water
    C. sand and broken stone
    D. sand, broken stone, and water

25. The head of a cold chisel has mushroomed after considerable use. The BEST thing to do is

   A. continue to use it since mushrooming is normal
   B. throw it away
   C. send it to the shop for redressing
   D. use a file to restore the head to its original shape

26. A valve box cover has been covered with asphalt during a street repaving job. The BEST way to locate the valve is to use a

   A. geophone
   B. aquaphone
   C. distribution map and a tape
   D. probing bar

27. The number of cubic yards in a bin 4 feet by 8 feet by 13 feet is MOST NEARLY _____ cubic yards.

   A. 17   B. 15   C. 13   D. 11

28. The letter *P* stencilled on the roadside face of a hydrant indicates that the hydrant

   A. is a low pressure hydrant
   B. is a high pressure hydrant
   C. is out of service permanently
   D. has a plugged drain

29. A hydrant extension piece would MOST likely be used if

   A. the hydrant had been damaged
   B. an open trench exists in the street in front of the hydrant
   C. several hose lines must be connected to the hydrant
   D. the hose connections do not fit the hydrant nozzles

30. The drip valve of a hydrant

   A. should not open until after the hydrant valve has closed
   B. should open just before the hydrant valve has closed
   C. operates completely independent of the operation of the hydrant valve
   D. should only be closed during repair of the hydrant

31. To remove and replace the operating parts of a hydrant which is in service,

   A. the standpipe must be disconnected from the elbow
   B. it is necessary to do some excavating
   C. the main must be shut down
   D. no excavation is necessary

32. The material generally used for packing hydrant stems is

   A. asbestos   B. rubber cloth
   C. flax   D. leather

33. A roundabout would normally have as a component part a

   A. four-way   B. valve   C. plug   D. cap

34. Cast iron reducers are usually made in all but one of the following ways. The way in which they are NOT made is

   A. spigots on both ends
   B. hub on large end, spigot on small end
   C. hub on small end, spigot on large end
   D. hubs on both ends

35. A cast iron main running due east is to turn so that it runs N45W, that is, halfway between north and west. The change in direction could be made using _____ bends.

   A. sixteen 1/48   B. six 1/16
   C. four 1/8   D. two 1/4

36. A cast iron offset would NORMALLY be used

   A. to change the direction of a main
   B. when the main must run diagonally from one side of the street to the other
   C. when the main must be shifted parallel to itself several feet to avoid an existing structure
   D. when the main must be shifted several inches to avoid an existing structure

37. A 30-inch cast iron main is to be laid with a blow-off and an air cock. The cast iron piece used for the blow-off differs from that used for the air cock in

   A. size of outlet
   B. general shape
   C. material used
   D. length measured along the main

38. The upper part of a standard hydrant valve box is USUALLY connected to the lower part by

   A. screw threads   B. bolts
   C. a beaded rim   D. lugs and rods

39. A trench for an 18-inch cast iron main is being excavated in rock. The width of the trench should be AT LEAST _____ inches.

   A. 30   B. 36   C. 42   D. 48

40. Specifications of the Department of Water Supply, Gas and Electricity state that in a trench excavated in rock, projections of rock must be removed if they come within a certain distance of the outside of any portion of the pipe barrel or bell. This distance is, in inches,

   A. 4   B. 6   C. 8   D. 10

KEY (CORRECT ANSWERS)

1. D	11. C	21. C	31. D
2. A	12. B	22. A	32. C
3. B	13. D	23. B	33. B
4. D	14. C	24. D	34. D
5. D	15. D	25. C	35. B
6. D	16. D	26. C	36. D
7. A	17. C	27. B	37. A
8. B	18. C	28. D	38. A
9. D	19. A	29. B	39. C
10. A	20. D	30. A	40. B

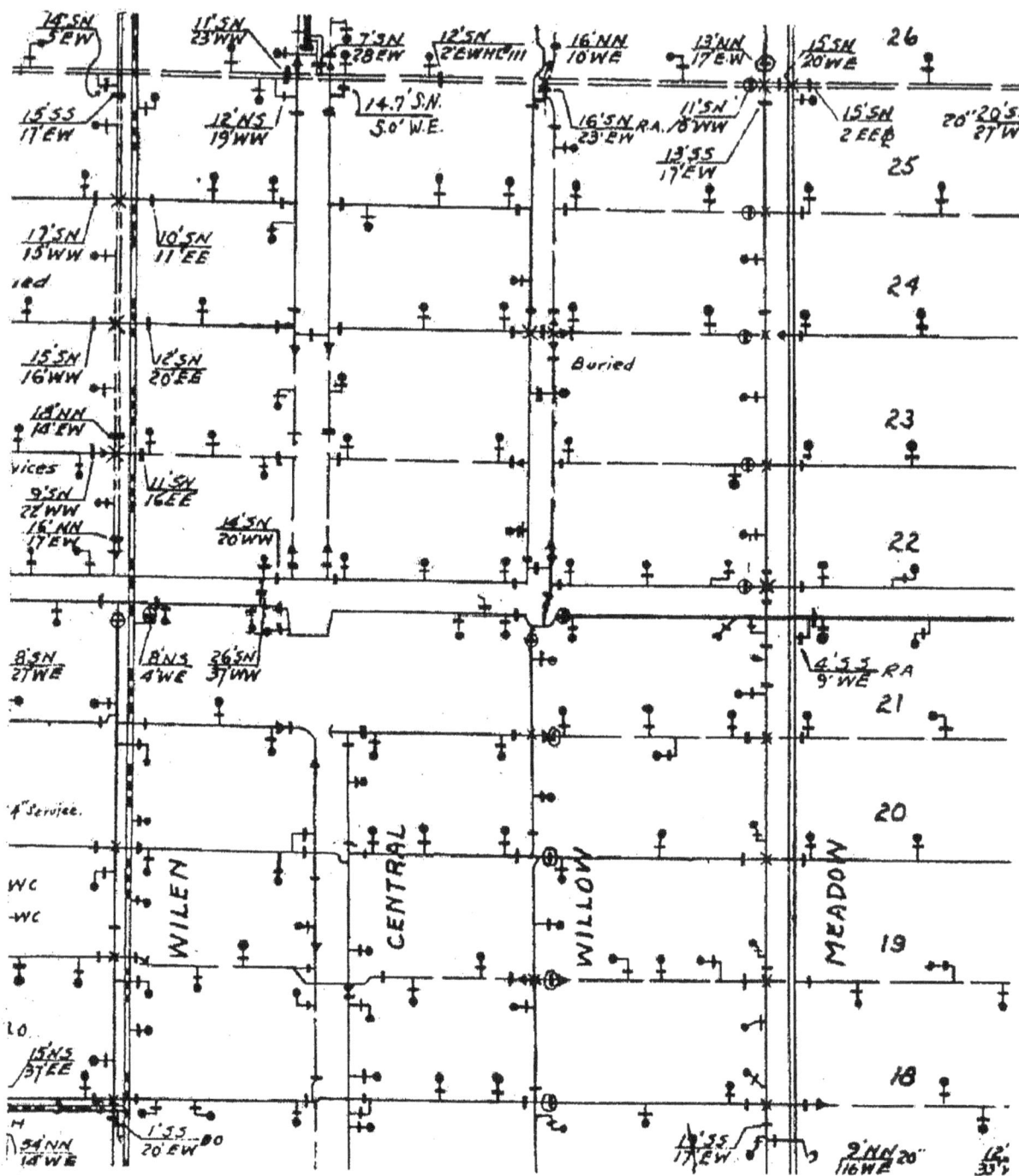

TEST 2

DIRECTIONS: Each question or incomplete statement is followed by several suggested answers or completions. Select the one that BEST answers the question or completes the statement. *PRINT THE LETTER OF THE CORRECT ANSWER IN THE SPACE AT THE RIGHT.*

1. The MAXIMUM size of stones permitted in backfill is _____ inches. 1____
   A. 12   B. 8   C. 4   D. 2

2. A two-inch galvanized steel pipe is to be connected to a cast iron main. 2____
   The connection should be made by a standard corporation tap of the following size: _____ inch.
   A. 1   B. 1 1/2   C. 2   D. 2 1/2

3. Standard cast iron pipe of inside diameter from 12 to 20 inches may be furnished in nominal laying lengths up to and including _____ feet. 3____
   A. 14   B. 16   C. 18   D. 20

4. The interior surface of new 12-inch cast iron pipe is USUALLY coated with 4____
   A. cement mortar   B. nothing
   C. asphalt paint   D. coal tar pitch

5. A tarpaulin would MOST likely be used when 5____
   A. mixing concrete
   B. running lead joints
   C. lowering pipe into a trench
   D. excavating a trench for a water main

6. Bands and bolts would be LEAST likely to be required at 6____
   A. bends   B. branches   C. plugs   D. four-ways

7. A house service with a 3/8-inch tap on an existing main is to be transferred to a new main. 7____
   The size of the tap on the new main should be _____ inch.
   A. 5/8   B. 1/2   C. 3/8   D. 1/4

8. The LARGEST tap permitted on a new 12-inch main is _____ inch. 8____
   A. 1   B. 1 1/2   C. 2   D. 2 1/2

9. The sheeting of a trench serves 9____
   A. only to protect workmen
   B. only to prevent damage to existing mains close to the trench
   C. only to prevent damage to pavement
   D. all three of the foregoing purposes

10. Water required for flushing backfill is USUALLY supplied

    A. in a fine spray
    B. by an ordinary garden hose
    C. from a tank truck
    D. through a flushing pipe

11. Water mains are USUALLY laid parallel to the curb at a distance of APPROXIMATELY _____ feet.

    A. 15   B. 12   C. 9   D. 6

12. After a main has been laid but prior to putting it into service, it should be disinfected by

    A. continuous flushing with water containing chlorine
    B. continuous flushing with clean water only
    C. introducing chlorine into the water in the pipe and letting the solution stand for 30 minutes
    D. blowing chlorine gas through the main

13. Before trimming a caulked pipe joint, the lead of a lead joint should

    A. extend outside the face of the bell
    B. be flush with the face of the bell
    C. be inside the face of the bell
    D. be heated

14. Drainage of hydrants require the use of lead lined pipe

    A. except when a cast iron drain base is provided
    B. except when the hydrant is connected to a sewer
    C. except when a blind drain is provided
    D. in every case

15. A standard cast iron reducer is to connect a 24-inch main to a smaller main. The length of the reducer USUALLY

    A. is the same regardless of the size of the smaller main
    B. decreases as the size of the smaller main decreases
    C. increases as the size of the smaller main decreases
    D. can be varied to fit the field conditions

16. A standard cast iron three-way does NOT have more than the following number of hubs:

    A. 3   B. 2   C. 1   D. 0

17. Of the following statements, the one which is CORRECT is:

    A. A cap is used on the spigot end of a pipe
    B. A plug is used on the spigot end of a pipe
    C. Caps and plugs can be used interchangeably
    D. Caps are usually available in larger sizes than plugs

18. Of the following statements, the one which is CORRECT is:

    A. A planned shutdown is not made rapidly
    B. In the event of an emergency shutdown, all valves in the area should be closed and then a study of the distribution map should be made to determine which valves can be opened
    C. Boundary gates should always be kept closed for the duration of an emergency shutdown
    D. The operation of all valves to be used in a planned shutdown should be checked prior to making the shutdown

19. When building material is stored on the street for the construction of a building,

    A. the Department of Water Supply, Gas and Electricity is not concerned
    B. there can be no objections if hydrants are accessible
    C. there can be no objections if the storage period is short
    D. serious difficulties for the Department of Water Supply, Gas and Electricity could result

20. A large steel main is to be emptied through a blow-off. The BEST way to proceed is to open

    A. the blow-off
    B. an aircock or hydrant at the high point of the main before opening the blow-off
    C. the blow-off and then open an air cock or hydrant at the high point of the main
    D. an air cock or hydrant at the low point of the main before opening the blow-off

21. A large new main is to be placed in service.
    To fill the main, it is important to FIRST open

    A. the head gate valve
    B. an air cock or hydrant on the main
    C. all side gate valves
    D. the side gate valves on one side of the main only

22. Of the following special castings, the one which is MOST like a blow-off is a

    A. four-way   B. reducer   C. three-way   D. offset

23. The laying length of a double hub

    A. is less than one foot
    B. depends upon the diameter of the pipe
    C. must be at least nine feet
    D. may be any length up to 20 feet, the maximum length depending upon the diameter

24. The gooseneck that is GENERALLY used to connect a service pipe to a main

    A. should be straight for its entire length
    B. comes in a standard length and, therefore, must be curved to make it fit

C. is deliberately curved so that it can accommodate movement between main and service pipe
D. is curved to provide extra length so that it can be cut and still be long enough to reconnect to the main

25. A non-rising stem gate valve would MOST likely be used when

   A. the threads of the stem must be readily accessible for lubrication
   B. space is limited
   C. the valve is used infrequently
   D. the valve is in a deep valve vault

26. Of the following types of valves, the one which is NOT usually found on water mains is the _____ valve.

   A. glove   B. air relief
   C. pressure regulating   D. gate

27. When a length of cast iron pipe is too long, it is USUALLY cut with a(n)

   A. chisel   B. hacksaw
   C. emery wheel   D. cutting torch

28. The PRINCIPAL objection to laying mains between December 15 and March 15 is with the

   A. freezing of water
   B. working conditions for the men
   C. freezing of soil
   D. the reduced length of daylight

29. A trench for a cast iron main is USUALLY backfilled immediately

   A. after the joints are caulked
   B. after the pressure test has been completed
   C. before water is placed in the main
   D. after water is placed in the main

30. When the pavement along the sides of a trench becomes undermined, the BEST thing to do is

   A. carefully tamp the backfill under the undermined pavement
   B. place a layer of broken stone on top of the backfill under the undermined pavement
   C. break down the undermined pavement before backfilling
   D. consolidate the backfill by thorough flushing

31. A small leak in a main would usually be MOST serious in the

   A. summer   B. fall   C. spring   D. winter

32. When sheeting for a trench is not to be removed before backfilling, the sheeting should be driven or cut off so that it

   A. is flush with the surface of the ground
   B. is at least 8 inches below the surface of the ground

C. will project at least two inches into the pavement base
D. is flush with the top surface of the pavement base

33. While excavating a trench in rock by blasting, a water main which crosses the line of the trench is uncovered. Of the following methods, the BEST one for continuing the rock excavation in the vicinity of the main is

   A. shut down the main
   B. place blasting mats to cover the main
   C. use lighter blasting charges
   D. relocate the main temporarily so that it is outside the danger area of the building

34. When the bottom of a trench for a water main is in rock, the pipe should be permanently supported on

   A. clean earth backfill which is tamped
   B. wooden blocking
   C. sand backfill which is flushed
   D. concreted cradles

35. On which one of the following days of the week should a planned shutdown normally be made?

   A. Sunday
   B. Monday
   C. Tuesday
   D. Wednesday

36. Permissible leakage during a field test is two (2) gallons per linear foot of pipe joint per 24 hours.
    For a 24-inch main, 1,000 feet long, with 16-foot laying lengths, the permissible leakage in 24 hours is, in gallons, MOST NEARLY

   A. 750   B. 770   C. 790   D. 810

37. Contract limitations on the maximum quantities of materials that may be delivered to the site, and on the time of such deliveries, are USUALLY made in order to

   A. insure the completion of the work on schedule
   B. prevent the contractor from asking for an extension of time because materials were not available
   C. reduce congestion at the site of the work
   D. protect the manufacturer supplying the material

38. Steel reinforcing bars for reinforced concrete should

   A. be painted with red lead
   B. be painted with asphalt paint
   C. be painted with oil paint
   D. not be painted

39. Steel water mains are lined with

   A. coal tar enamel only
   B. coal tar enamel or cement mortar
   C. cement mortar only
   D. nothing

40. The principal danger in NOT opening an air cock when draining a main is that the main might

    A. not empty
    B. only partly empty
    C. empty too fast
    D. collapse

KEY (CORRECT ANSWERS)

1. C	11. C	21. B	31. D
2. B	12. A	22. C	32. B
3. D	13. A	23. A	33. D
4. A	14. D	24. C	34. D
5. C	15. C	25. B	35. D
6. D	16. B	26. A	36. C
7. A	17. A	27. A	37. C
8. C	18. D	28. C	38. D
9. D	19. D	29. A	39. B
10. D	20. B	30. C	40. D

EXAMINATION SECTION
TEST 1

DIRECTIONS: Each question or incomplete statement is followed by several suggested answers or completions. Select the one that BEST answers the question or completes the statement. *PRINT THE LETTER OF THE CORRECT ANSWER IN THE SPACE AT THE RIGHT.*

1. A Bourdon tube gage is used to measure

    A. temperature
    B. acidity
    C. turbidity
    D. pressure

    1.____

2. An instrument used to locate buried metallic pipes is known as a(n)

    A. scleroscope
    B. M-scope
    C. kinoscope
    D. oscilloscope

    2.____

3. The PRIMARY function of a check valve is to

    A. prevent the illegal use of fire hydrants
    B. insure adequate water pressure in high buildings
    C. prevent freezing of water
    D. permit flow of water in one direction only

    3.____

4. Of the following, the torque applied by a ratchet wrench would be expressed in units of

    A. horsepower
    B. pounds
    C. pounds per square inch
    D. foot-pounds

    4.____

5. Most lead joints runners are made of

    A. nylon
    B. asbestos
    C. leadite
    D. polyethylene

    5.____

6. The tool shown in the sketch at the right is a

    A. pickout iron
    B. pipe jointer
    C. cover bolt wrench
    D. pipe reamer

    6.____

7. In order to reduce the force necessary to open or close large gate valves, the valves are equipped with a

    A. vacuum breaker
    B. by-pass
    C. saddle
    D. shear gate

    7.____

8. In order to open a ground-key valve, used as a corporation cock to full flow, it is necessary to rotate the handle _____ degrees.

    A. 45   B. 60   C. 75   D. 90

    8.____

27

9. A foot valve is MOST often used

   A. to relieve excess pressure in a water main
   B. on the suction pipe of a centrifugal pump
   C. at the high point in a pipeline
   D. to drain a pipeline

10. Of the following tools, the one that generally should NOT be used to tighten screwed piping is a _____ wrench.

    A. Stillson
    B. strap
    C. monkey
    D. chain

11. A 6-inch branch may be connected to an 8-inch main without shutting off the flow of water by using a

    A. tapping valve and sleeve
    B. cutting in tee
    C. cutting in valve and sleeve
    D. pipe tong

12. When water flows through a thirty-second bend, the direction of flow changes

    A. 11 1/4°   B. 22 1/2°   C. 45°   D. 90°

13. A main in which water is flowing east is connected to a pipe offset. As the water leaves the offset, it will be flowing toward the

    A. north   B. south   C. east   D. west

14. An electrolysis test connection on a water main is used to measure the

    A. salinity of the ground water outside the main
    B. the chlorine residual in the water in the main
    C. stray electric current in the main
    D. temperature of the ground around the main

15. A common method of temporarily lowering the ground water below the level of operations in a trench is by the use of

    A. wellpoints
    B. mud valves
    C. piles
    D. trenching machines

16. The diameter of a #6 steel reinforcing bar is MOST NEARLY

    A. 1"   B. 3/4"   C. 1/2"   D. 1/4"

17. The quick opening or closing of valves or gates, and the sudden starting, stopping, or variation in speed of pumps is FREQUENTLY the cause of

    A. sluggish flow of water
    B. water-borne diseases
    C. water hammer
    D. water hardness

18. Poured lead pipe joints must be calked MAINLY because the hot lead

    A. corrodes some of the cast iron
    B. burns some of the jute
    C. becomes porous on cooling
    D. shrinks on cooling

19. Flexibility between a water main and a service pipe can be obtained by the use of a   19.____

    A. corporation cock	B. gooseneck
    C. curb stop	D. air-release valve

20. It is necessary to shut off the water in a main temporarily in order to make repairs.   20.____
    In order to get cooperation from the general public, the

    A. job should be done at night so that few people will be aware of it
    B. shut-off crew should be ordered not to speak to the general public
    C. job should be done in several stages so that the public realizes how difficult the problem is
    D. purpose and duration of the shut-off should be explained to the general public

Questions 21-25.

DIRECTIONS: Questions 21 through 25 are to be answered on the basis of maps or diagrams used by departments of water resources.

21. On a distribution map, the symbol ———— — ———— refers to a main whose diameter is   21.____

    A. 6"	B. 8"	C. 10"	D. 12"

22. On a distribution map, the symbol ⌀ refers to a   22.____

    A. gate valve	B. blow-off
    C. air-cock	D. regulator

23. On a distribution map, the symbol ——|—— refers to a   23.____

    A. gate valve	B. 3-way
    C. 4-way	D. reducer

24. On a distribution map, the symbol ↓ refers to a   24.____

    A. hydrant	B. air-cock	C. 3-way	D. 4-way

25. On a work area diagram, the symbol ▨ refers to a(n)   25.____

    A. office	B. truck
    C. barricade	D. excavation.

KEY (CORRECT ANSWERS)

1.	D	11.	A
2.	B	12.	A
3.	D	13.	C
4.	D	14.	C
5.	B	15.	A
6.	D	16.	B
7.	B	17.	C
8.	D	18.	D
9.	B	19.	B
10.	C	20.	D

21. B
22. B
23. A
24. C
25. D

TEST 2

DIRECTIONS: Each question or incomplete statement is followed by several suggested answers or completions. Select the one that BEST answers the question or completes the statement. *PRINT THE LETTER OF THE CORRECT ANSWER IN THE SPACE AT THE RIGHT.*

1. According to standard water main specifications, prior to laying any straight pipe or special castings, the inside surfaces shall be mopped or sprayed with a chlorine solution containing not less than 150 _____ of chlorine.

    A. quarts   B. lbs.   C. p.p.m.   D. tanks

2. When water main repairs are underway on the north side of a two-way street which runs east and west, the location recommended by the Department of Water Resources of a lead heating burner is _____ of the excavation.

    A. north   B. east   C. south   D. west

3. Of the following statements, the one which is NOT included on the official water supply shut-off notice is

    A. turn off water-cooled refrigerating and air conditioning units
    B. close main house valve on water pipe supplying premises
    C. drain all water pipes above the basement
    D. open, as a vent, one hot water faucet above the level of the hot water storage tank

4. In order to obtain a Temporary Street Opening Permit, the applicant must be a

    A. city resident   B. city employee
    C. licensed plumber   D. professional engineer

5. In accordance with standard water main specifications, all water mains 20 inches in diameter or larger shall be subjected to a leakage test at a pressure of 125 psi. The leakage shall NOT be greater than

    A. twenty gallons per 24 hours
    B. two gallons per linear foot of pipe joint per 24 hours
    C. two gallons per linear foot of pipe joint per 20 minutes
    D. twenty gallons per mile of pipe per 24 hours

6. In accordance with official specifications, in paved streets the length of trench that may be opened between the point where the backfilling has been completed and the point where the pavement is being removed shall NOT exceed

    A. the width of the street
    B. fifteen hundred feet for pipes 24 inches or less in diameter
    C. five hundred feet for all pipe diameters
    D. the distance between hydrants

Questions 7-10.

DIRECTIONS: Questions 7 through 10 are to be answered SOLELY on the basis of the following passage.

The choice of equipment to be used in excavating a trench will depend on the job conditions, the depth and width of the trench, the class of the soil, the extent to which ground water is present, the width of the right of way for the disposal of excavated earth, and the type of equipment already owned by a contractor.

If a relatively shallow and narrow trench is to be excavated in firm soil, the wheel-type trenching machine is probably the most suitable. However, if the soil is rock, which requires blasting, the most suitable excavator will be a hoe, or a less desirable substitute could be a dragline. If the soil is unstable, water-saturated material, it may be necessary to use a dragline, hoe, or clamshell and let the walls establish a stable slope. If it is necessary to install solid sheeting to hold the walls in place, neither a hoe nor a dragline will work satisfactorily. A clamshell, which can excavate between the trench braces that hold the sheeting in place, probably will be the best equipment for the job.

7. According to the above passage, the wheel-type trenching machine is probably the MOST suitable for excavating

   A. unstable, water-saturated material
   B. when it is necessary to install solid sheeting
   C. a relatively shallow and narrow trench in firm soil
   D. when ground water is present

8. According to the above passage, the width of the right of way for the disposal of excavated earth

   A. depends upon the width of the street
   B. affects the depth of cover
   C. affects the choice of equipment to be used in excavating
   D. should be minimized to avoid inconveniencing the public

9. According to the above passage, a hoe will be the MOST suitable excavator if the

   A. soil is rock which requires blasting
   B. equipment is already owned by a contractor
   C. trench requires solid sheeting
   D. trench is over twenty feet deep

10. According to the above passage, the BEST equipment to use for excavating when it is necessary to install solid sheeting to hold the walls in place probably will be a

    A. clamshell
    B. dragline
    C. hoe
    D. wheel-type trenching machine

Questions 11-12.

DIRECTIONS: Questions 11 and 12 are to be answered SOLELY on the basis of the following passage.

Construction pumps frequently are required to perform under severe conditions, such as resulting from variations in the pumping head or from handling water that is muddy, sandy and trashy, or highly corrosive. The rate of pumping may vary several hundred percent during the period of construction. The most satisfactory solution to the pumping problem may be a single all-purpose pump, or it may be to use several types and sizes of pumps, to permit flexibility in the operations. The proper solution is to select the equipment which will take care of the pumping needs adequately at the lowest total cost.

11. According to the above passage, the PROPER solution to a construction pumping problem is to select equipment that has the lowest total cost which will also

    A. perform under severe conditions
    B. take care of the pumping needs adequately
    C. permit flexibility in operations
    D. provide maximum safety

12. According to the above passage, a variation of several hundred percent during the period of construction may occur in the

    A. pumping head
    B. rate of pumping
    C. volume of sandy and trashy water
    D. volume of highly corrosive water

Questions 13-14.

DIRECTIONS: Questions 13 and 14 are to be answered SOLELY on the basis of the following passage.

The mechanical failure of equipment may be the cause of a serious accident. Competent maintenance of equipment will reduce mechanical failures and in so doing reduce injuries and construction interruptions. Regular inspection of equipment will reduce maintenance expense.

13. Of the following, the BEST title for the above passage is

    A. Construction Productivity
    B. Preventive Maintenance of Equipment
    C. Inspection of Equipment
    D. Economical Construction

14. According to the above passage, the way to save money in construction work is to

    A. have qualified people operate equipment
    B. have periodic inspection of equipment
    C. have regular overhaul of equipment
    D. start a maintenance training program

15. Of the following items, the one MOST suitable for measuring the flow of water in a pipe is a

    A. poppet   B. hydraulic ram
    C. cistern   D. pitometer

16.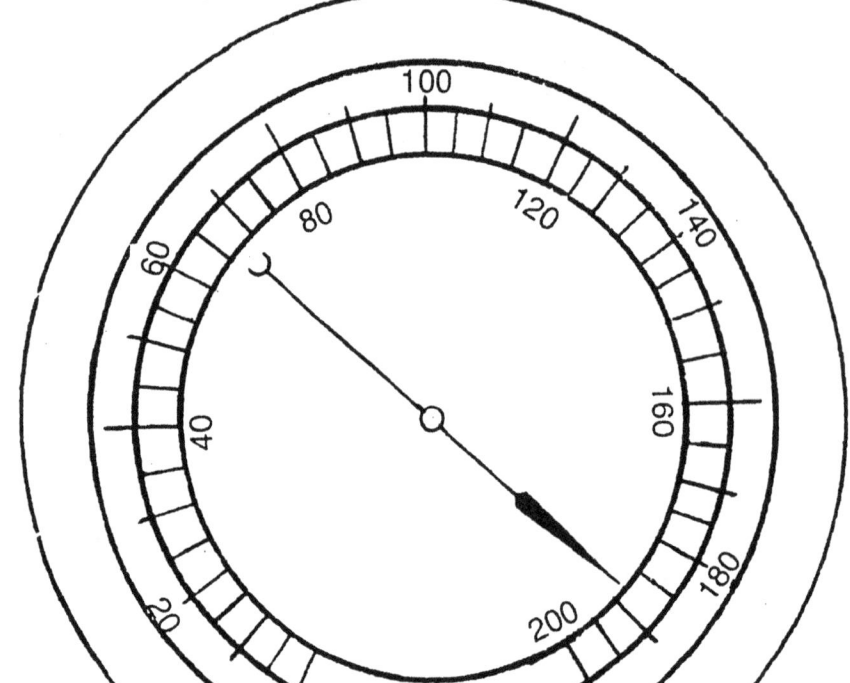

BOURDON DIAL

The reading indicated on the above dial is MOST NEARLY

A. 183 B. 188 C. 192 D. 196

17. An instrument used for detecting the sound of flowing water in a pipe network is a(n)

A. micrometer
B. spectrometer
C. aquaphone
D. viscophone

18. Of the following, the MAIN purpose of a Venturi meter is to measure the _____ in a main.

A. quantity of water flowing
B. chlorine content of the water
C. velocity of the water
D. temperature of the water

19. A blade with a small hole in the tip, used for measuring the flow from a hydrant, is a

A. hydrant pitot
B. Venturi meter
C. parshall flume
D. hydrant head

20. Hydrant-flow tests include observation of the pressure at a centrally situated hydrant and measurement of

   A. pressure at a group of neighboring hydrants
   B. flow from outlets at the top floor of a building
   C. reservoir elevation
   D. flow from a group of neighboring hydrants

21. Of the following, the one which is NOT a requirement of a satisfactory report is that it should be

   A. timely   B. lengthy   C. legible   D. accurate

22. When an accident occurs, the FIRST concern of the Foreman should be to

   A. see that injured person is properly cared for
   B. make sketches of the area
   C. interview the injured person
   D. interview witnesses and coworkers

23. Workers whose characteristics and behavior are such as to make them considerably more liable to injury than the average person are considered to be

   A. late
   B. safety conscious
   C. careful
   D. accident-prone

24. Safety inspections are not useful in an accident prevention program unless

   A. all persons who have accidents are fined
   B. insurance rates are decreased
   C. immediate action is taken to correct the conditions revealed
   D. there is adequate compensation for all injured parties

25. A Foreman is BEST qualified to investigate accidents involving his subordinates because he

   A. has all safety equipment for the job
   B. has more free time than his superiors
   C. has more skill than his superiors
   D. is familiar with all the job conditions

KEY (CORRECT ANSWERS)

1.	C	11.	B
2.	D	12.	B
3.	C	13.	B
4.	C	14.	B
5.	B	15.	D
6.	B	16.	B
7.	C	17.	C
8.	C	18.	A
9.	A	19.	A
10.	A	20.	D

21. B
22. A
23. D
24. C
25. D

EXAMINATION SECTION
TEST 1

DIRECTIONS: Each question or incomplete statement is followed by several suggested answers or completions. Select the one that BEST answers the question or completes the statement. *PRINT THE LETTER OF THE CORRECT ANSWER IN THE SPACE AT THE RIGHT.*

1. Of the following methods of installing pipe in a trench, the one which is MOST acceptable is to

    A. use a flat bottom trench and backfill not tamped
    B. have pipe supported on blocks and backfill tamped
    C. use a flat bottom trench and backfill tamped
    D. have pipe supported on blocks, backfill not tamped

    1.____

2. When cutting a 30" diameter cast iron pipe, it is BEST to use a(n)

    A. cold chisel
    B. diamond point chisel
    C. hardy
    D. ordinary wheel type of cutter

    2.____

3. Of the following materials, the one which is BEST suited for yarning bell and spigot joints on water pipe is

    A. plumber's yarn
    B. boatmaker's yarn
    C. tar impregnated oakum
    D. sterilized yarn

    3.____

4. A valve that is used between low pressure and high pressure areas in water distribution systems is called a boundary valve.

    A. pressure reducing
    B. check
    C. gate
    D. globe

    4.____

5. Cast iron pipe is particularly adapted to underground and submerged service because of its

    A. ease in handling and joining
    B. high corrosion-resisting qualities
    C. ability to withstand high pressures
    D. low first cost

    5.____

6. In caulking a pipe joint, excessive *caulking* should be avoided to prevent

    A. *thinning* the lead
    B. a second pouring of lead
    C. *misses*
    D. bell damage

    6.____

7. The material used to disinfect water pipes before and after laying the pipe is USUALLY

    A. chlordane
    B. calcium chloride
    C. chlorine
    D. washing soda

    7.____

8. Of the following items, the one that is NOT a component part of a mechanical joint is a(n)

   A. yarn
   B. gland
   C. rubber gasket
   D. socket

9. Of the following causes of water leaks in mains, the one that is LEAST common is

   A. improper caulking
   B. poor backfilling
   C. improper handling of pipe
   D. manufacturing defects in the pipe

10. The BEST type of wrench to use for making up a mechanical joint in cast iron pipe is a _____ wrench.

    A. ratchet   B. monkey   C. strap   D. Stillson

11. The MAIN difference between skeleton sheathing and tight sheathing is that in skeleton sheathing

    A. a greater part of the sheathing is omitted
    B. reinforced laced type of sheathing is used
    C. the rangers and braces are placed differently
    D. no planks are used

12. The width of the trench at each caulking joint, in comparison with the remaining portion of the trench, should generally be

    A. equal to twice the diameter of the pipe to allow for caulking
    B. of sufficient size to allow for caulking
    C. equal to the diameter of the pipe plus 12 inches
    D. equal to the diameter of the pipe plus 1/2 pipe radius

13. Unless otherwise directed, a trench for a water pipe line should USUALLY be excavated to a depth of 4 feet measured from the surface of the roadway to the _____ of the pipe.

    A. center   B. bottom   C. invert   D. top

14. The length of trench excavation for the installation of a 30-inch pipe should NOT exceed _____ feet.

    A. 1500   B. 1300   C. 1100   D. 1000

15. Before laying a new water main, test pits or test trenches may be necessary in order to determine

    A. the amount of materials required
    B. subsurface obstructions
    C. the proper width of excavation
    D. the amount of labor needed

16. The outside circumference of a pipe that has an outside diameter of 11 1/2" is MOST NEARLY

    A. 32"   B. 36"   C. 39"   D. 42"

17. Continuous sheathing is USUALLY used when excavating a trench in

    A. unstable soil
    B. firm earth
    C. stiff clay
    D. rock

18. Assume that a pump is pumping water out of an excavated trench at the rate of 30 gallons per minute.
    The time that is required to pump 2700 gallons of water out of this trench would be MOST NEARLY _____ hour(s).

    A. 4 1/2   B. 3   C. 1 1/2   D. 3/4

19. The size of *rangers* that should be used for trenches dug to a depth of seven (7) feet is APPROXIMATELY

    A. 1" x 2"   B. 2" x 3"   C. 2" x 4"   D. 4" x 6"

20. The bottom of wood sheathing is USUALLY

    A. squared on all sides
    B. steel tipped in order to penetrate hard material
    C. capped in order to prevent splintering
    D. bevelled on both one face and one edge

21. The quickest and easiest way of disconnecting a bell and spigot lead joint in a pipe is by

    A. using a picking chisel at the joint
    B. cracking the bell
    C. melting the lead at the joint with an acetylene torch
    D. using a diamond point chisel

22. A joint runner is USUALLY used as a

    A. guide for molten lead
    B. scab on sheathing
    C. clamp for two pipes
    D. filler between pavement joints

23. Of the following tools, the one which is NOT usually used for caulking a joint is the

    A. stub
    B. regular
    C. cold chisel
    D. diamond joint

24. The type of lead USUALLY used to caulk cast iron pipe joints in water mains is

    A. lead wool
    B. shredded lead
    C. leadite
    D. pure soft lead

25. The distance that a *ranger* is USUALLY placed below the surface of a roadway is APPROXIMATELY

    A. 12"   B. 10"   C. 8"   D. 6"

26. The proper manner to unload cast iron pipe at a trench site which is APPROXIMATELY 300 feet long is to

   A. stack it at convenient locations
   B. stack it in even layers with 4" x 4" stringers between each layer with blocks at each end
   C. lay it along the route with the bell facing in the direction in which the work is to proceed
   D. store it where it will not collect rain water and be damaged in freezing weather

27. Damage to cast iron pipe may sometimes result from rough handling when in transit. A simple method of determining whether the pipe was damaged or not is to

   A. *ring* each length with a hammer
   B. drop the pipe to see if it breaks
   C. hydraulically test the pipe
   D. visually examine the pipe for cracks

28. A blowoff connection in a water distribution main is USUALLY located at the

   A. highest point of the line
   B. lowest point of the line
   C. midway point between two distribution mains
   D. center line of the pipe

29. The proper depth of lead joints for a 4" or 6" cast iron pipe is MOST NEARLY _____ inches.

   A. 3 1/2   B. 3 1/4   C. 3   D. 2 3/8

30. The distance that fire hydrants should be located back from the face of the curb line is MOST NEARLY

   A. 6-10"   B. 12-16"   C. 18-20"   D. 22-26"

31. Your orders to your crew are MOST likely to be followed if you

   A. explain the reasons for these orders
   B. warn that all violators will be punished
   C. promise easy assignments to those who follow these orders best
   D. say that they are for the good of the department

32. In order to be a good supervisor, you should

   A. impress upon your men that you demand perfection in their work at all times
   B. avoid being blamed for your crew's mistakes
   C. impress your superior with your ability
   D. see to it that your men get what they are entitled to

33. In giving instructions to a crew, you should

   A. speak in as loud a tone as possible
   B. speak in a coaxing persuasive manner
   C. speak quietly, clearly, and courteously
   D. always use the word *please* when giving instructions

34. The BEST procedure to follow when a difficult and unusual problem arises involving the laying of a water pipe is to   34.____

    A. ask another pipe caulker for his opinion
    B. proceed working in the usual manner
    C. report the situation to the engineer
    D. continue working, making necessary changes yourself

35. Assume that you are in charge of a crew making repairs on a water main. A bystander whom you do not know begins to comment on the way the work is being done. He makes several suggestions which he claims will result in a better job.   35.____
    Of the following, you should

    A. hold up the work until you can discuss the suggestions with your superior
    B. listen to him, thank him, and proceed with the work as you have been doing
    C. tell him to go along about his own business since you can do the job without any advice
    D. tell him to take his comments and suggestions to your superior who has the authority to change procedure

36. Assume that a pipe worker earns $16,625 per year. If seventeen percent of his pay is deducted for taxes, social security, and pension, his net weekly pay will be APPROXIMATELY   36.____

    A. $319.70   B. $300.80   C. $290.60   D. $265.00

37. If eighteen (18) feet of 4" cast iron pipe weighs approximately 390 pounds, the weight of this pipe per lineal foot will be MOST NEARLY _____ lbs.   37.____

    A. 19   B. 21   C. 23   D. 25

38. A one-sixteenth cast iron fitting will change the direction of water APPROXIMATELY   38.____

    A. 90°   B. 45°   C. 22 1/2°   D. 11 1/4°

39. The overall length of a standard cast iron bell-and-spigot water pipe is MOST NEARLY   39.____

    A. 10' 4 1/2"   B. 11'9"   C. 12' 4 1/2"   D. 20'0"

40. In rock excavations, the minimum depth that rock must be removed from the bottom of the bell of a cast iron pipe to the bottom of a trench should be MOST NEARLY   40.____

    A. 3"   B. 4"   C. 6"   D. 9"

KEY (CORRECT ANSWERS)

1. C	11. A	21. C	31. A
2. B	12. B	22. A	32. D
3. D	13. D	23. D	33. C
4. C	14. D	24. D	34. C
5. B	15. B	25. A	35. B
6. D	16. B	26. C	36. D
7. C	17. A	27. A	37. B
8. A	18. C	28. B	38. C
9. D	19. D	29. D	39. C
10. A	20. D	30. C	40. C

TEST 2

DIRECTIONS: Each question or incomplete statement is followed by several suggested answers or completions. Select the one that BEST answers the question or completes the statement. *PRINT THE LETTER OF THE CORRECT ANSWER IN THE SPACE AT THE RIGHT.*

1. If four (4) men are *backfilling* a trench, the proper number of men for *tamping* should usually be NOT LESS than 1._____

    A. 2 B. 4 C. 6 D. 8

2. A subsurface leak in a street main may be located by means of a(n) 2._____

    A. amprobe
    B. aquaphone
    C. aqueduct
    D. drill rod

3. The FIRST step in shutting off a water main in a street is to 3._____

    A. close the blowoff and notify the Department of Public Works
    B. close the blowoff and notify the Police Department
    C. notify the householders and the Fire Department
    D. close the head gates and notify the Fire Department

4. Concentric reducers are used for 4._____

    A. maintaining the same center line elevation
    B. keeping the bottom of the pipe at the same level
    C. changing the direction of flow in a pipe
    D. lowering the inverts of the pipe

5. A valve box is generally built with an open bottom so that 5._____

    A. the valve box can rest directly on the pipe
    B. the valve can be removed rapidly
    C. any water seeping into it will drain away
    D. a bottom connection can be made

6. If lead that is being used for caulking is overheated, it will be found that the caulked lead ring from a joint would MOST likely be 6._____

    A. too soft B. porous C. brittle D. flexible

7. A pipe compound used for making up threaded joints USUALLY acts as a filler between the threads and also as a 7._____

    A. hardener
    B. lubricant
    C. cleanser
    D. coolant

8. By referring to a concrete mix having a ratio of 1:2:4 is meant that the ingredients are made up of 1 part _____, 2 parts _____, and 4 parts _____. 8._____

    A. cement; sand; gravel
    B. sand; cement; water
    C. gravel; sand; cement
    D. sand; cement; gravel

9. The total weight of materials (lead and hemp) used in caulking an 8" bell and spigot joint for water is MOST NEARLY _____ lbs.

   A. 7 B. 10 C. 15 D. 24

10. Assume that a length of cast iron pipe measures 9'8" and three pieces of pipe are to be cut from this pipe, one 2'9", the second 3'2", and the third 1'10".
    The amount of pipe remaining after making these cuts (assuming no waste) is MOST NEARLY

    A. 1'6" B. 1'9" C. 1'11" D. 2'2"

11. Of the following types of valves, the one that is used to permit the flow of water in one direction is the _____ valve.

    A. gate B. angle C. globe D. check

12. Water mains in the city are generally located APPROXIMATELY _____ feet from the _____ line.

    A. four (4); curb
    B. five (5); sewer
    C. six (6); building
    D. nine (9); curb

13. Of the following equipment, the one which a pipe worker is NOT normally required to know how to operate is the

    A. backhoe
    B. air-powered chipping hammers and caulking tools
    C. various types of pipe laying derricks
    D. air-powered pavement breakers and rock drills

14. Assume that, after installing a mechanical joint in a water main, a leak occurs around the joint.
    Of the following, the BEST practice to follow would be to

    A. retighten the bolts
    B. loosen the bolts to expand the rubber gasket
    C. *hammer* home the spigot into the bell
    D. disassemble the joint, clean thoroughly, and reassemble

15. It is a good policy to keep excavated material away from the edge of a trench a distance of AT LEAST

    A. 2 feet B. 18 inches C. 1 foot D. 6 inches

16. Neglecting friction, the height, in feet, to which water can rise having a pressure of 55 pounds per square inch is MOST NEARLY

    A. 120 B. 150 C. 180 D. 210

17. If it takes 3 men 11 days to dig a trench, the number of days it will take 5 men to dig the same trench, assuming all work is done at the same rate of speed, is MOST NEARLY

    A. 6 1/2 B. 7 3/4 C. 8 1/4 D. 8 3/4

18. It is sometimes found that poured lead joints tend to crack open due to shrinkage. This is USUALLY due to

    A. overheating of the lead
    B. impurities in the lead
    C. excessive pressure at the joint
    D. cooling of the lead

19. The BEST material to use for backfilling trenches that are made in rock is USUALLY

    A. tan bark B. cinders C. gravel D. sand

20. For an average pipe repair job, it is the practice to use a gang made up of

    A. one pipe caulker and three laborers
    B. two pipe caulkers and three laborers
    C. one supervisor, two pipe caulkers, and two laborers
    D. three laborers and two helpers

21. Slack in cables or tie rods is USUALLY *taken up* by the use of

    A. drift pins
    B. clamps
    C. Crosby clips
    D. turnbuckles

22. A pneumatic tool is one that is USUALLY directly operated by means of

    A. gasoline
    B. compressed air
    C. oil pressure
    D. electricity

23. The BEST thing to do when a pavement breaker becomes jammed in the pavement is to

    A. attempt to work it loose without using another breaker
    B. shut off the air compressor
    C. increase the air supply
    D. use another pavement breaker to cut it loose

24. If a trench is dug 6'0" deep, 2'6" wide, and 8'0" long, the area of the opening, in square feet, is MOST NEARLY

    A. 48 B. 32 C. 20 D. 15

Questions 25-30.

DIRECTIONS: Questions 25 through 30 are to be answered in accordance with the sketch shown on the following page, which represents a portion of a water distribution map and other facilities.

4 (#2)

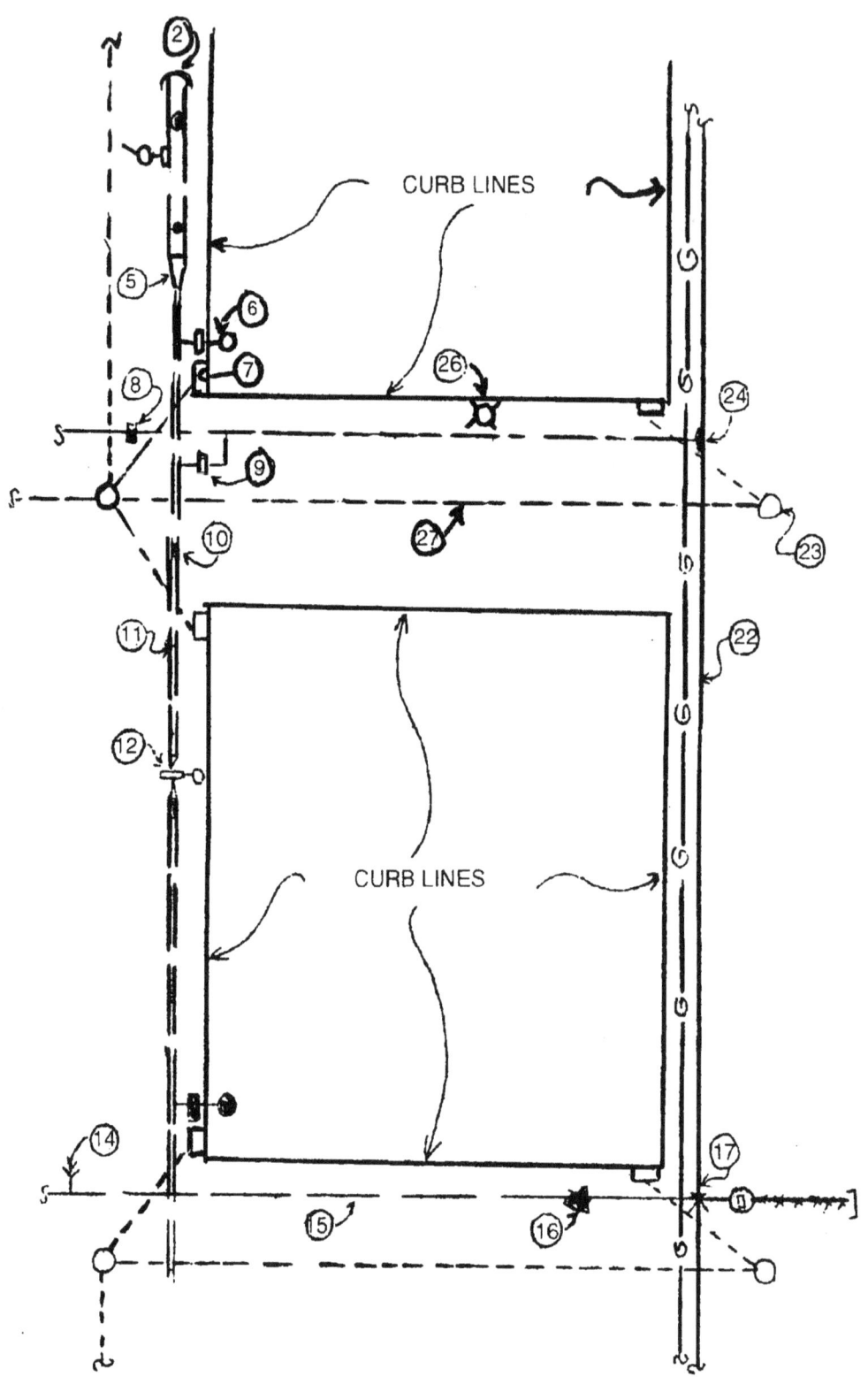

The above sketch represents a portion of a water distribution map and other facilities. To be used in answering questions numbered 25 to 30 inclusive.

5 (#2)

25. A hydrant symbol is numbered 25.____
    A. 26 B. 14 C. 6 D. 9

26. A cap symbol is numbered 26.____
    A. 2 B. 5 C. 9 D. 10

27. Of the following numbered lines, the one which is NOT a water line is numbered 27.____
    A. 11 B. 15 C. 22 D. 27

28. A reducer symbol is numbered 28.____
    A. 8 B. 16 C. 12 D. 14

29. A catch basin symbol is numbered 29.____
    A. 7 B. 10 C. 23 D. 24

30. A valve symbol is numbered 30.____
    A. 17 B. 14 C. 10 D. 8

31. Opening a fire hydrant near the high point of a newly installed portion of a water main, prior to testing, is USUALLY done in order to remove 31.____
    A. air   B. obstructions
    C. slime growths   D. P. mineral deposits

32. Taps, or wet connections to a city main, may be made by 32.____
    A. a licensed plumber
    B. the Department of Water Supply, Gas and Electricity
    C. the Department of Public Works
    D. any experienced laborer

33. The supervisor made a ridiculous statement. As used in this sentence, the word ridiculous means MOST NEARLY 33.____
    A. incorrect B. evil C. unfriendly D. foolish

34. That pipe caulker is engaged in a hazardous job. As used in this sentence, the word hazardous means MOST NEARLY 34.____
    A. inconvenient   B. dangerous
    C. difficult   D. demanding

35. Breaks in water distribution mains are front page news for the very reason that they occur infrequently. As used in this sentence, the word infrequently means MOST NEARLY 35.____
    A. at regular intervals B. often
    C. rarely   D. unexpectedly

36. Several kinds of self-caulking substitutes for lead have been developed. As used in this sentence, the word substitutes means MOST NEARLY 36.____
    A. additives   B. replacements
    C. hardeners   D. softeners

37. Cast iron is <u>essentially</u> an alloy of iron and carbon. As used in this sentence, the word <u>essentially</u> means MOST NEARLY 37.____

    A. never   B. basically   C. barely   D. sometimes

38. A pipe worker sometimes makes a <u>trivial</u> mistake. As used in this sentence, the word <u>trivial</u> means MOST NEARLY 38.____

    A. common   B. significant
    C. obvious   D. unimportant

39. When water moves through pipe, <u>friction</u> is developed between the water and the inside surface of the pipe. As used in this sentence, the word <u>friction</u> means MOST NEARLY 39.____

    A. resistance   B. heat
    C. slippage   D. pressure

40. Assume that a piece of cast iron pipe has to be cut to fit between two cast iron bells fixed in place in a trench. Of the following statements, the one which is MOST NEARLY correct is that, if the pipe is cut too 40.____

    A. short, the next joint may have to be broken to make up the difference
    B. short, the yarn used for caulking might be pushed through past the end of the pipe
    C. long, the proper amount of caulking lead could not be used at the joints
    D. long, the joint would need a bottom support

KEY (CORRECT ANSWERS)

1. B		11. D		21. D		31. A
2. B		12. D		22. B		32. B
3. C		13. A		23. D		33. D
4. A		14. D		24. C		34. B
5. C		15. A		25. C		35. C
6. C		16. A		26. A		36. B
7. B		17. A		27. D		37. B
8. A		18. D		28. B		38. D
9. C		19. D		29. A		39. A
10. C		20. A		30. D		40. B

EXAMINATION SECTION
TEST 1

DIRECTIONS: Each question or incomplete statement is followed by several suggested answers or completions. Select the one that BEST answers the question or completes the statement. *PRINT THE LETTER OF THE CORRECT ANSWER IN THE SPACE AT THE RIGHT.*

1. If cast iron weighs 450 pounds per cubic foot, the weight of a solid cast iron manhole cover 2 feet in diameter and 1 inch thick is MOST NEARLY _____ pounds.

    A. 94 B. 118 C. 136 D. 164

2. A gas which has an odor similar to rotten eggs is

    A. argon
    C. nitrogen
    B. phosgene
    D. hydrogen sulfide

3. The gases released by digesting sewage sludges contain about 72%

    A. methane B. chlorine C. helium D. copper

4. In sewer maintenance, an orange peel bucket is USUALLY used for

    A. testing for toxic gases
    C. cleaning roof drains
    B. rodding sewers
    D. cleaning catch basins

5. A plumbing device that prevents the passage of bad odors and gases from the sewer system to a building is a

    A. corporation stop
    C. curb box
    B. union
    D. trap

6. An 8-inch diameter sewer enters at the upstream side of a manhole, and a 10-inch sewer leaves at the downstream side. The crowns of the sewers are at the same elevation. If the invert elevation of the 8-inch sewer is 100.64 feet, the invert elevation of the 10-inch sewer is MOST NEARLY _____ feet.

    A. 100.32 B. 100.41 C. 100.47 D. 100.52

7. Where ground slopes are unfavorable, it is necessary to keep sanitary sewer grades at the minimum velocity that will prevent the settling of material when the sewer is flowing full.
The velocity is MOST NEARLY _____ feet per second.

    A. 0.2 B. 2.0 C. 20.0 D. 200.0

8. A condition that will permit polluted water to enter a potable water supply is a

    A. tide gate
    C. cathodic protection
    B. cross connection
    D. reducer

9. A wheel with a grooved rim, such as is mounted in a pulley block to guide rope or cable, is a

    A. turnbuckle
    C. slant
    B. wormgear
    D. sheave

10. A device used in a combined sewer to bypass excess storm-flow is a(n)

    A. soffit
    B. side-flow weir
    C. aquafer
    D. cellular cofferdam

11. A device installed at the discharge end of a sewer outfall which operates to permit gravity flow at low stages in the receiving waters, but closes to prevent backflow when the elevation of the receiving waters is high, is a

    A. flume
    B. buttress
    C. tide gate
    D. flocculator

12. A pipe used to carry streamflow under a highway embankment is a

    A. culvert   B. lock   C. standpipe   D. pitot

13. The pipe on the discharge side of a sewage pump is a

    A. tell-tale pipe
    B. sump pipe
    C. suction pipe
    D. force main

14. A model 6520 sewer cleaner is rated at 60 GPM at 1000 PSI. As used here, PSI is an abbreviation for

    A. positive surging inflow
    B. per sewer invert
    C. pounds per square inch
    D. pounds per sewer inlet

15. In order to increase culvert efficiency and to prevent undermining of the culvert, the entrance to the culvert is FREQUENTLY provided with a

    A. sump pump
    B. mud valve
    C. head wall
    D. scroll case

16. A sewer plan calls for pipe diameters of 3", 10", 12", 14", 15", and 18". The size which is NOT used for a standard strength clay sewer pipe is

    A. 10"   B. 12"   C. 14"   D. 15"

17. Lateral sanitary sewers should PREFERABLY intersect at a

    A. catch basin
    B. weir
    C. manhole
    D. tide gate

18. A dip, or sag, used in a sewer line to pass under structures, such as subways, is called a(n)

    A. outfall
    B. inverted siphon
    C. force main
    D. regulator

19. A device suitable for pumping sewage from deep basements into city sewers is a

    A. pressure relief valve
    B. vacuum breaker
    C. pneumatic ejector
    D. comminutor

20. The flow of ground water into sanitary sewers through defective joints is called

    A. back siphonage
    B. infiltration
    C. overflow
    D. exfiltration

KEY (CORRECT ANSWERS)

1.	B	11.	C
2.	D	12.	A
3.	A	13.	D
4.	D	14.	C
5.	D	15.	C
6.	C	16.	C
7.	B	17.	C
8.	B	18.	B
9.	D	19.	C
10.	B	20.	B

TEST 2

DIRECTIONS: Each question or incomplete statement is followed by several suggested answers or completions. Select the one that BEST answers the question or completes the statement. *PRINT THE LETTER OF THE CORRECT ANSWER IN THE SPACE AT THE RIGHT.*

1. In a combined sewer system, the amount of sewage flowing to the treatment plant is USUALLY controlled by a

    A. regulator
    B. bar screen
    C. siphon
    D. mud valve

2. The LOWEST portion of the inside of a sewer pipe is the

    A. crown
    B. haunch
    C. invert
    D. spring line

3. A.C. pipe, sometimes used instead of clay sewer pipe, is made of

    A. reinforced concrete
    B. polyvinyl
    C. asbestos and cement
    D. asphalt

4. Of the following, the one which is NOT a sewer cleaning tool is the

    A. gouge
    B. wire brush
    C. pilaster
    D. claw

5. A sewer rodding machine has speeds up to 100 FPM. As used here, FPM is an abbreviation for feet per

    A. million B. mile C. minute D. module

6. The nominal diameter of a #4 reinforcing bar is MOST NEARLY

    A. 0.4" B. 0.04" C. 0.5" D. 4 mm

7. In a 1:2:3 concrete mix, the number 3 represents the proportion of

    A. sand
    B. water
    C. coarse aggregate
    D. cement

8. Of the following, a procedure used for causing air to flow into and from the lungs of the body by mechanical or manual methods is called

    A. irrigation
    B. traction
    C. traumatic shock
    D. artificial respiration

9. The one of the following that is a toxic gas which is colorless and odorless is

    A. chlorine
    B. hydrogen sulfide
    C. carbon monoxide
    D. gasoline

10. In first aid, a tourniquet is MOST often used to

    A. improve respiration
    B. treat burns
    C. treat sprains
    D. control bleeding

11. Persons who have been injured may suffer a depressed condition of many of the body functions due to failure of enough blood to circulate through the body.
    This condition is called

    A. immunization B. chronic
    C. cathartic D. shock

12. The type of injury which is MOST likely to cause lockjaw (tetanus) is

    A. an epileptic convulsion B. a puncture wound
    C. an electric shock D. sunstroke

13. Wellpoints are used in sewer construction PRIMARILY to

    A. remove gases B. dewater trenches
    C. locate wells D. replace hydrants

14. A sewer which carries only sewage from the plumbing fixtures in a house is a

    A. storm sewer B. combined sewer
    C. sanitary sewer D. subsurface drain

15. The slope of a sewer is MOST usually indicated by the units,

    A. feet B. rods C. percent D. diameters

16. Longitudinal timbers used to support the vertical sheeting in a sewer trench excavation are called

    A. wales B. cross braces
    C. piles D. cradles

17. The sum of 2 5/8, 3 3/16, 1 1/2, and 4 1/4 is

    A. 9 13/16 B. 10 7/16 C. 11 9/16 D. 13 3/16

Questions 18-20.

DIRECTIONS: Questions 18 through 20 should be answered by selecting the word that MOST NEARLY means the SAME as the word in capital letters.

18. SUPPLEMENT

    A. terminal B. absence C. addition D. void

19. HAZARDOUS

    A. dense B. safe C. dangerous D. high

20. VERIFY

    A. climb B. travel C. slide D. confirm

KEY (CORRECT ANSWERS)

1.	A	11.	D
2.	C	12.	B
3.	C	13.	B
4.	C	14.	C
5.	C	15.	C
6.	C	16.	A
7.	C	17.	C
8.	D	18.	C
9.	C	19.	C
10.	D	20.	D

EXAMINATION SECTION
TEST 1

DIRECTIONS: Each question or incomplete statement is followed by several suggested answers or completions. Select the one that BEST answers the question or completes the statement. *PRINT THE LETTER OF THE CORRECT ANSWER IN THE SPACE AT THE RIGHT.*

1. To check for the entrance of toxic wastes into a treatment plant, each of the following may be reliably observed as indicators EXCEPT

   A. changes in color of incoming wastewater
   B. waste recording equipment
   C. odors
   D. bulking of sludge in the clarifier

   1.____

2. An increase in _____ could cause a demand for more oxygen in an aeration tank.

   A. inert or inorganic wastes
   B. pH
   C. toxic substances
   D. microorganisms

   2.____

3. Chlorine may be added for hydrogen sulfide control in the

   A. collection lines   B. aeration tank
   C. plant effluent   D. trickling filter

   3.____

4. The range of typical carrying capacities, in gallons per minute, of intermediate pumping stations is

   A. less than 600   B. 200-700
   C. 100-1,600   D. 700-10,000

   4.____

5. A low sulfanator injector vacuum reading could be caused by

   A. missing gasket
   B. high back pressure
   C. high-volume injector flow
   D. wrong orifice

   5.____

6. Before starting a rotating biological contactor process, each of the following should be checked EXCEPT

   A. lubrication   B. biomass
   C. clearance   D. tightness

   6.____

7. The capacity for water or wastewater to neutralize acids is expressed in terms of

   A. pH   B. oxygen demand
   C. alkalinity   D. acidity

   7.____

8. Which of the following is NOT one of the available methods for determining stormwater flow for the purpose of storm sewer design?

   8.____

A. Rainfall and runoff correlation studies
B. Inlet method
C. Hydrograph method
D. Outlet method

9. What is the term for the accumulation of residue that appears on trickling filters and must be removed periodically?

   A. Sludges   B. Slurries   C. Slugs   D. Sloughings

10. A sludge containing a high number of living organisms is referred to as

    A. raw   B. activated   C. primary   D. toxic

11. Which of the following is NOT a plant location where liquid mixing is commonly practiced?

    A. Ponds
    B. Hydraulic jumps in open channels
    C. Pipelines
    D. Venturi flumes

12. Which of the following industries releases primarily inorganic wastes in its effluent?

    A. Paper   B. Petroleum
    C. Gravel washing   D. Dairy

13. Which of the following collection system variables could upset a plant's activated sludge process?

    A. Discharge by industrial cleaning operations
    B. Chlorination of return sludge flows
    C. Decreases in influent flows
    D. Recycling of digester supernatant

14. The second-stage BOD is also referred to as the _____ stage.

    A. carbonaceous   B. pretreatment
    C. flocculation   D. nitrification

15. When organic matter decomposes to form foul-smelling products associated with the lack of free oxygen, this condition is known as

    A. shock loading   B. septicity
    C. sloughing   D. sidestreaming

16. Which type of bacteria has the HIGHEST optimum temperature for treatment?

    A. Mesophilic   B. Cryophilic
    C. Thermophilic   D. Psychrophilic

17. The COD test

    A. estimates the total oxygen consumed
    B. measures the carbon oxygen demand
    C. provides results more quickly than the BOD test
    D. measures only the nitrification oxygen demand

18. Which of the following is NOT considered a major factor that may cause variations in lab test results?　　18.____

    A. The nature of the material being examined
    B. Testing equipment
    C. Sampling procedures
    D. The quantity of material being examined

19. The treatment process that MOST effectively removes suspended solids from wastewater is　　19.____

    A. sedimentation　　　　　　　　B. flocculation
    C. skimming　　　　　　　　　　　D. comminution

20. Which of the following is a thickening alternative in sludge processing?　　20.____

    A. Flotation　　　　　　　　　　　B. Incineration
    C. Elutriation　　　　　　　　　　D. Wet oxidation

21. The device that continuously adds the flow of wastewater into a plant is the　　21.____

    A. aggregate　　　　　　　　　　　B. turbidity meter
    C. titrator　　　　　　　　　　　　D. totalizer

22. Two types of measurement required in connection with the operation of a treatment plant are　　22.____

    A. effluent and downstream
    B. temperature and dissolved oxygen
    C. in-plant and receiving water
    D. temperature and receiving water

23. You may NOT dispose of excess activated sludge waste from package plants　　23.____

    A. at a nearby treatment plant
    B. by anaerobic digestion
    C. by removal by septic tank pumper
    D. by aeration in a holding tank, then deposit in a sanitary landfill

24. What is the term for the combination of activated sludge with raw wastewater in a treatment plant?　　24.____

    A. Median　　　　　　　　　　　　B. Liquefaction
    C. Effluent　　　　　　　　　　　　D. Mixed liquor

25. Landfills produce poisonous _____ gas as a byproduct of decomposition.　　25.____

    A. methane　　　　　　　　　　　　B. nitrogen
    C. chlorofluorocarbons　　　　　　D. argon

KEY (CORRECT ANSWERS)

1. B
2. D
3. A
4. D
5. B

6. B
7. C
8. D
9. D
10. B

11. A
12. C
13. A
14. D
15. B

16. C
17. C
18. D
19. B
20. A

21. D
22. C
23. B
24. D
25. A

TEST 2

DIRECTIONS: Each question or incomplete statement is followed by several suggested answers or completions. Select the one that BEST answers the question or completes the statement. *PRINT THE LETTER OF THE CORRECT ANSWER IN THE SPACE AT THE RIGHT.*

1. Which of the following types of pumps is a kinetic pump?　　　　　　　　　　　　　　　　1.____

   A. Rotary
   C. Hydraulic ram
   B. Piston plunger
   D. Blow case

2. What device is used to keep floated solids out of the effluent in dissolved air flotation thickeners?　　　2.____

   A. Cloth screens
   C. Effluent baffles
   B. Microscreens
   D. Water sprays

3. The _____ is NOT one of the primary factors affecting the flow of wastewater and sewage in sewers.　　　3.____

   A. viscosity of the liquid
   B. cross-sectional area of the system conduit
   C. time of day
   D. pipe surface

4. What is the term for washing a digested sludge in the plant effluent?　　　　　　　　　　　　4.____

   A. Masking
   C. Hydrolysis
   B. Elutriation
   D. Slaking

5. _____ is NOT an objective in periodically pumping sludge from the primary clarifier to the digester.　　　5.____

   A. Prevention of pump clogging
   B. Prevention of digester overload
   C. Allowance for thicker sludge pumping
   D. Maintenance of good clarifier conditions

6. The toxic chemical LEAST likely to be encountered by treatment plant operators is(are)　　　　6.____

   A. mercury
   C. fluorocarbons
   B. acids
   D. bases

7. Which concentration of total dissolved solids, in milligrams per liter, would be the MINIMUM required in order to be considered *strong* in wastewater?　　　7.____

   A. 250　　　B. 500　　　C. 850　　　D. 1,200

8. What is the term for the treatment process in which a tank or reactor is filled, the water is treated, and the tank is emptied?　　　8.____

   A. Flocculation
   C. Batch process
   B. Centration
   D. Pond process

9. The mixing of a compound with water to produce a true chemical reaction is to　　　　　　9.____

   A. dissolve　　　B. slake　　　C. strip　　　D. hydrate

10. If the difference in elevation between inflow and outflow sewers is greater than 1.5 feet, which device is needed?

    A. Side weir
    B. Drop inlet
    C. Baffles
    D. Inlet casting

11. Intermittent releases or discharges of industrial wastes are known as

    A. slurries   B. slugs   C. splashes   D. stop logs

12. Results from the settleability test of activated sludge solids may be used to

    A. calculate BOD
    B. determine probable flow rates at which sludges may clog equipment
    C. calculate sludge age
    D. determine ability of solids to separate from liquid in final clarifier

13. The device used to measure the temperature of an effluent is a

    A. thermometer
    B. Bourdon tube
    C. thermocouple
    D. pug mill

14. Which source is typically the HEAVIEST contributor of total solids in a service area's wastewater supply?

    A. Industrial wastes
    B. Domestic wash waters
    C. Storm runoff
    D. Human biological wastes

15. The term for liquid removed from a settled sludge is

    A. hydrolyte
    B. supernatant
    C. aliquot
    D. slurry

16. A unit of wastewater moving through the treatment system without dispersing or mixing with the rest of the wastewater in the system is called

    A. centration
    B. plug flow
    C. putrefaction
    D. slugging

17. What is the term for the groups or clumps of bacteria or particles that have clustered together during the treatment process?

    A. Coagulants
    B. Slurries
    C. Floes
    D. Slugs

18. The purpose of PRIMARY sedimentation is to remove

    A. settleable and floatable material
    B. roots, rags, and large debris
    C. suspended and dissolved solids
    D. sand and gravel

19. _____ would NOT cause an increase in effluent coliform levels at a treatment plant.

    A. Mixing problems
    B. An increase in effluent BOD
    C. Solids accumulation in the contact chamber
    D. High chlorine residual

20. What is the term used to describe bacteria that can live under either aerobic or anaerobic conditions? 20.____

    A. Cultured
    B. Agglomerated
    C. Filamentous
    D. Facultative

21. Which devices are NOT used during pretreatment? 21.____

    A. Racks
    B. Comminutors
    C. Screens
    D. Coagulators

22. Through which stage in an activated sludge treatment plant would wastewater pass FIRST? 22.____

    A. Grit chambers
    B. Bar racks
    C. Settling tanks
    D. Primary sedimentation

23. The inorganic gas LEAST likely to be found around a treatment plant is 23.____

    A. ammonia
    B. methane
    C. hydrogen sulfide
    D. mercaptans

24. The soils in an effluent disposal on land program may be tested using each of the following procedures EXCEPT 24.____

    A. BOD
    B. conductivity
    C. pH
    D. cation exchange capacity

25. Which of the following is a conditioning alternative in sludge processing? 25.____

    A. Centrifugation
    B. Drying
    C. Composing
    D. Elutriation

KEY (CORRECT ANSWERS)

1. C		11. B	
2. C		12. D	
3. C		13. C	
4. B		14. A	
5. A		15. B	
6. C		16. B	
7. C		17. C	
8. C		18. A	
9. B		19. D	
10. B		20. D	

21. D
22. B
23. D
24. A
25. D

EXAMINATION SECTION
TEST 1

DIRECTIONS: Each question or incomplete statement is followed by several suggested answers or completions. Select the one the BEST answers the question or completes the statement. *PRINT THE LETTER OF THE CORRECT ANSWER IN THE SPACE AT THE RIGHT.*

1. In general, the most economic means of removing excess copper from water is

    A. reverse osmosis
    B. ion exchange
    C. lime softening
    D. coagulation/filtration

    1.____

2. The EPA's rules on sampling for coliforms require a minimum standard sampling volume of _____ ml.

    A. 50
    B. 100
    C. 200
    D. 500

    2.____

3. Which of the following processes typically occurs LATEST in the water treatment sequence?

    A. Activated carbon treatment
    B. Eutrophication control
    C. Flocculation
    D. Iron/Manganese control

    3.____

4. In terms of water quality, "true color" refers to the color of a sample

    A. under ultraviolet light
    B. of raw water
    C. that has undergone direct filtration
    D. with turbidity removed

    4.____

5. What is considered to be a reasonable range of concentration (mg/L) for iodine in drinking water?

    A. 0.5-1.0
    B. 10-12
    C. 75-150
    D. 250-600

    5.____

6. Which of the following disinfecting agents involves the danger of explosive tendency?

    A. Chloramine
    B. Ozone
    C. Sodium hypochlorite
    D. Chlorine dioxide

    6.____

7. When the alkalinity of a water sample is less than the hardness, the existing salts of calcium and magnesium are likely to be

   A. sulfates instead of carbonates
   B. bicarbonates
   C. carbonates instead of sulfates
   D. negligible

8. Which of the following coagulants is often used in the treatment of very cold water?

   A. Hydrated lime
   B. Filter alum
   C. Activated silica
   D. Sodium aluminate

9. After the initial agitation, controlled agitation for coagulation should be maintained at a rate of about _____ ft/sec.

   A. 0.1-0.3
   B. 0.2-0.6
   C. 0.5-2.0
   D. 3.0-5.0

10. According to the federal Criteria for Evaluation and Standards Specifications, which of the following is classified as a Type A inorganic chemical?

    A. Sodium
    B. Tin
    C. Copper
    D. Iron

11. Which of the following should NEVER be added before lime soda softening or ion exchange?

    A. Polyelectrolytes
    B. Fluoride compound
    C. Activated alumina
    D. Chlorine compound

12. The usual process for the removal of iron and manganese from water is

    A. Aeration
    B. Downflow granular filtration
    C. Sedimentation
    D. Coagulation/flocculation

13. Turbidity is a characteristic mostly caused by the presence of _____ matter in water.

    A. ionized
    B. crystalloid
    C. molecular
    D. colloidal

14. Ideally, filter backwashing should be scheduled on the basis of

    A. volume treated
    B. time
    C. head loss
    D. post-filtration contamination

15. According to federal regulations, any water beneath the surface of the ground with significant and rapid shifts in characteristics such as turbidity, temperature, pH, or conductivity with closely correlates to climatological conditions is defined as

    A. contaminated water
    B. groundwater above the water table
    C. groundwater under the direct influence of surface water
    D. raw water

16. For taste and odor control, powdered activated carbon is normally introduced

    A. before aeration
    B. after softening
    C. before coagulation
    D. after filtration

17. In the context of water treatment, the most important sodium compound found in water is

    A. borax
    B. sodium phosphate
    C. sodium bicarbonate
    D. common salt (sodium chloride)

18. If volatile organic compounds are not detected in groundwater, the EPA still requires source testing every

    A. quarter
    B. year
    C. 3 years
    D. 5 years

19. Organic substances such as humic and fulvic acids are coagulated by

    A. soda ash
    B. calcite and polyelectrolytes
    C. iron and aluminum salts
    D. bentonite or Fuller's earth

20. Which of the following compounds has the lowest maximum contaminant level (MCL, in mg/L) assigned by the EPA?

    A. Glyphosate
    B. Xylene
    C. Benzene
    D. Dioxin

21. To prevent the formation of currents and breaking of floc during settling, the overflow rate should not exceed _____ gal/day/ft of weir length.

    A. 170
    B. 540
    C. 12,300
    D. 20,000

22. Which of the following chemicals has some nutritional value in small quantities?

    A. Arsenic
    B. Cadmium
    C. Nitrate
    D. Lead

23. In a raw water with a concentration of 100-300 mg/L of suspended solids, a 50% removal is typically accomplished with a detention time during sedimentation of _____ hour(s).

    A. 0.5-1.0
    B. 1.0-1.5
    C. 2.0-4.0
    D. 4.0-6.0

24. According to Standard Methods, which of the following tests is an appropriate method of analysis for disinfection by-products?

    A. Volumetric method
    B. Combustible-gas indicator method
    C. Micro liquid-liquid extraction gas chromatography
    D. Purge-and-trap gas column gas chromatography

25. The use of fine screens in drawing raw water from pretreatment storage serves to intercept large and fine solids, and involves the additional advantage of

    A. moderate aeration
    B. lowering organic content
    C. enhancing the life of filters
    D. improving the efficiency of coagulation

KEY (CORRECT ANSWERS)

1.	C	11.	B
2.	B	12.	A
3.	D	13.	D
4.	D	14.	C
5.	A	15.	C
6.	B	16.	C
7.	A	17.	D
8.	D	18.	D
9.	C	19.	C
10.	C	20.	D

21. D
22. A
23. B
24. C
25. D

TEST 2

DIRECTIONS: Each question or incomplete statement is followed by several suggested answers or completions. Select the one the BEST answers the question or completes the statement. *PRINT THE LETTER OF THE CORRECT ANSWER IN THE SPACE AT THE RIGHT.*

1. The operation of a public water supply system is

   A. recorded and reported daily
   B. recorded daily and reported monthly
   C. recorded weekly and reported monthly
   D. recorded and reported monthly

   1.____

2. The most commonly used dechlorinating agent, both in treatment and sampling, is

   A. sodium thiosulfate
   B. acetone
   C. calcium carbonate
   D. chlorine dioxide

   2.____

3. Which of the following substances, at a low concentration, will impart a swampy, musty odor to drinking water?

   A. Hydrogen sulfide
   B. E. coli
   C. Calcium carbonate
   D. Lead

   3.____

4. Which of the following traditional treatment processes contributes the most to corrosion in the distribution system?

   A. Water softening
   B. Coagulation/Flocculation
   C. Sedimentation
   D. Aeration

   4.____

5. Which of the following terms is an expression of the concentration of calcium and magnesium ions in water?

   A. Turbidity
   B. Alkalinity
   C. Settleable solids
   D. Hardness

   5.____

6. The most effective coagulants for the removal of viruses from raw water are typically

   A. copperas and chlorinated copperas
   B. silica and clays
   C. lime and calcite
   D. alum and ferric chlorides

   6.____

7. The Platinum-Cobalt Method is a means of

   A. ionization
   B. standardizing color
   C. reducing hardness
   D. fixing pH value

8. Generally, flow through settling basins should be maintained at or under _____ ft/sec.

   A. 0.5
   B. 1
   C. 3
   D. 5

9. Which of the following is NOT a process for removing turbidity from drinking water?

   A. Aeration
   B. Filtration
   C. Sedimentation
   D. Coagulation

10. Sampling program subdivisions routinely include each of the following, EXCEPT

    A. sampling points indicative of pretreatment, intermediate, and post-treatment
    B. distribution sampling
    C. raw water sampling
    D. biomatter sampling

11. The major consumer of chlorine in the first stage of disinfection is

    A. ammonia
    B. ozone
    C. free hydrogen
    D. sodium hydroxide

12. Which of the following is NOT a recommended treatment process for the removal of mercury?

    A. Reverse osmosis
    B. Activated alumina adsorption
    C. Granular activated carbon
    D. Lime softening

13. The processes available for desalination include each of the following, EXCEPT

    A. reverse osmosis
    B. ion exchange
    C. lime softening
    D. electrodialysis

14. What is the EPA's published maximum contaminant level goal (MCLG, in mg/L), for sulfate?

    A. 0.500
    B. 5.000
    C. 50.00
    D. 500.0

15. The EPA's rules on sampling for coliforms state under normal circumstances (when more than 40 samples per month are taken) state that not more than _____ sample(s) per month may be positive.

    A. 1
    B. 2
    C. 5
    D. 10

16. Which of the following statements about the lime-soda softening process is TRUE?

    A. A reduced feeding velocity is usually necessary.
    B. Disinfection by chlorination of softened water must be increased.
    C. Only brief flocculation is necessary.
    D. Sedimentation times between 1-2 hours are sufficient.

17. Which of the following treatment processes will have an effect on the barium level of a water supply?

    A. Rapid sand filtration
    B. Aeration
    C. Lime softening
    D. Coagulation

18. Which of the following coagulants is generally considered ineffective for colored waters?

    A. Copperas
    B. Calcite or whiting
    C. Ferric sulfate
    D. Clay

19. The most practical time to increase the chlorination of a water supply is

    A. after filtration and before chemical treatment
    B. at the effluent or final chlorination
    C. after chemical treatment but before fluoridation
    D. after settling and before filtration

20. The porosity of gravels used in rapid sand filters should remain between _____ %.

    A. 10-20
    B. 35-45
    C. 40-60
    D. 75-85

21. Which of the following chemicals' content in water is regulated by the EPA?

    A. Potassium
    B. Phosphorus
    C. Bromine
    D. Magnesium

4 (#2)

22. Under EPA's "Phase I" requirements, initial sampling of a surface or groundwater source is required   22.____

    A. monthly
    B. quarterly
    C. biannually
    D. annually

23. Typically, filter washwater will account for about _____ % of the totalplant flow.   23.____

    A. 2-4
    B. 8-10
    C. 15-22
    D. 20-30

24. Which of the following is NOT a process in the disinfection of raw water that can eliminate trihalomethanes (THMs) such as chloroform?   24.____

    A. Coagulation
    B. Activated carbon
    C. Aeration
    D. Ozonation

25. The control of coagulation in the treatment process is significantly affected by each of the following, EXCEPT   25.____

    A. dissolved oxygen
    B. turbidity
    C. free carbon dioxide
    D. pH

KEY (CORRECT ANSWERS)

1.	B	11.	A
2.	A	12.	B
3.	A	13.	C
4.	D	14.	D
5.	D	15.	C
6.	D	16.	B
7.	B	17.	C
8.	A	18.	A
9.	A	19.	D
10.	D	20.	B

21. C
22. B
23. A
24. A
25. A

TEST 3

DIRECTIONS: Each question or incomplete statement is followed by several suggested answers or completions. Select the one the BEST answers the question or completes the statement. *PRINT THE LETTER OF THE CORRECT ANSWER IN THE SPACE AT THE RIGHT.*

1. Which of the following processes is LEAST likely to be included in a solids-contact unit? 1.____

   A. Sedimentation
   B. Flocculation
   C. Rapid mixing
   D. Filtration

2. Water with applicable concentrations of 150-300 mg/L would be described as 2.____

   A. soft
   B. moderately hard
   C. hard
   D. very hard

3. Which of the following is a method of adsorption? 3.____

   A. Osmosis
   B. Iron/manganese removal
   C. Filtration
   D. Activated carbon treatment

4. Typically, the temperature of water sampled for a Taste Threshold Test should be at about _____ °C. 4.____

   A. 15
   B. 30
   C. 45
   D. 60

5. Under the EPA's Phase II rules, sampling for asbestos must occur 5.____

   A. once, during the first year only
   B. once each year for surface water and once every three years for groundwater
   C. quarterly for the first year, annually after that, and then every 3 years if not detected
   D. quarterly for the first year, reduced to one per year after one round of no detection

6. Following mixing, operational limits generally require a detention time for coagulation and flocculation of between 6.____

   A. 10-15 minutes
   B. 15-45 minutes
   C. 1-2 hours
   D. 3-4 hours

7. pH values higher than 7 are generally expected in samples of raw water due to the presence of

   A. carbonates and bicarbonates
   B. oxides
   C. nitrates
   D. microbes

8. Which of the following chemicals has been assigned a maximum contaminant level goal (MCLG) by the EPA?

   A. Dissolved oxygen
   B. Calcium
   C. Ozone
   D. Iron

9. In general, multiple chlorination is effective when the quality of raw water is good--but the factor of safety is

   A. fluoridation
   B. coagulation/flocculation
   C. filtration
   D. pH control

10. Which of the following coagulants is effective in absorbing taste and odor substances?

    A. Hydrated lime
    B. Copperas
    C. Bentonite
    D. Filter alum

11. Which of the following is generally considered to me the most effective method for the removal of nitrates from water?

    A. Biological denitrification
    B. Lime softening
    C. Chemical coagulation
    D. Anion exchange

12. For coagulation, the generally-accepted minimum alkalinity of water under treatment is about _____ mg/L as $CaCO_3$.

    A. 5
    B. 10
    C. 20
    D. 40

13. In-plant analyses reveal a sulfate level that is unacceptably high. As a first and most economical alternative, the plant should consider

    A. dilution from other water supply sources
    B. reverse osmosis
    C. ion exchange
    D. the use of aluminum sulfate in the coagulation/flocculation process

14. Which of the following existing plant operations can help to achieve a goal of trihalomethane (THM) reduction at a relatively low cost?
    I. Improved coagulation and settling through flocculant aids
    II. Chlorine dioxide treatment
    III. More frequent jar testing
    IV. Ozonation

    A. I and III
    B. I, II and IV
    C. III and IV
    D. I, II, III and IV

14.____

15. Which of the following is NOT typically used for pH adjustments to potable water?

    A. Soda ash
    B. Sodium silicate
    C. Caustic soda
    D. Lime

15.____

16. Which of the following physical parameters is a primary drinking water standard, as used by the EPA?

    A. Turbidity
    B. Corrosivity
    C. pH
    D. Total dissolved solids

16.____

17. The settling process is desirable for waters with a turbidity of _____ ppm or more.

    A. 10
    B. 30
    C. 50
    D. 100

17.____

18. Which of the following types of water analyses requires the use of a glass sampling bottle?

    A. Settleable matter
    B. Oil and grease
    C. Cyanides
    D. Conductance

18.____

19. The preferred method for the detection of cadmium in a water supply is the _____ method.

    A. Neocuproine
    B. Atomic Absorption Spectrometric
    C. Colorimetric
    D. Dithizone

19.____

20. The *primary* advantage associated with the use of sodium hypochlorite for disinfection is that it

    A. is odorless
    B. requires less storage space than most other compounds
    C. is safer to handle than most other compounds
    D. is stored dry

20.____

21. For which of the following is evidence of carcinogenicity the strongest?

    A. Styrene
    B. PCBs
    C. Toluene
    D. Arsenic

21.____

22. The expected residual of free chlorine at the end of a distribution is about _____ mg/L.

    A. .002
    B. 2
    C. 20
    D. 200

22.____

23. Because of its oxidation process and the consequent power to be virucidal, _____ is often a preferred disinfectant in the prechlorination process.

    A. Ozone
    B. Carbon dioxide
    C. Sodium thiosulfate
    D. Bromine

23.____

24. The fastest standardized method for the detection of coliforms is the

    A. presence-absence (P-A) coliform test
    B. membrane filter technique (MF)
    C. minimal media (MMO-MUG) test
    D. multiple-tube fermentation technique (MPN)

24.____

25. Which of the following is a precipitation treatment?

    A. Deferrization
    B. Fluoridation
    C. Flocculation
    D. Activated carbon treatment

25.____

KEY (CORRECT ANSWERS)

1. D	11. D
2. C	12. C
3. D	13. A
4. A	14. A
5. A	15. B
6. B	16. A
7. A	17. C
8. D	18. B
9. C	19. B
10. C	20. C

21. B
22. B
23. A
24. B
25. A

EXAMINATION SECTION
TEST 1

DIRECTIONS: Each question or incomplete statement is followed by several suggested answers or completions. Select the one that BEST answers the question or completes the statement. *PRINT THE LETTER OF THE CORRECT ANSWER IN THE SPACE AT THE RIGHT.*

Questions 1-5.

DIRECTIONS: Questions 1 through 5 consist of sentences, each of which contains one underlined word whose meaning you are to identify by marking your answer either A, B, C, or D.

EXAMPLE

Public employees should avoid <u>unethical</u> conduct.
The word unethical, as used in the sentence, means MOST NEARLY
   A. fine   B. dishonest   C. polite   D. sleepy
The correct answer is *dishonest* (B). Therefore, you should mark your answer B.

1. Employees who can produce a <u>considerable</u> amount of good work are very valuable.
   The word *considerable*, as used in the sentence, means MOST NEARLY
      A. large   B. potential   C. necessary   D. frequent

   1._____

2. No person should <u>assume</u> that he knows more than anyone else.
   The word *assume*, as used in the sentence, means MOST NEARLY
      A. verify   B. hope   C. suppose   D. argue

   2._____

3. The parties decided to <u>negotiate</u> through the night.
   The word *negotiate*, as used in the sentence, means MOST NEARLY
      A. suffer   B. play   C. think   D. bargain

   3._____

4. Employees who have <u>severe</u> emotional problems may create problems at work.
   The word *severe*, as used in the sentence, means MOST NEARLY
      A. serious   B. surprising   C. several   D. common

   4._____

5. Supervisors should try to be as <u>objective</u> as possible when dealing with subordinates.
   The word *objective*, as used in the sentence, means MOST NEARLY
      A. pleasant   B. courteous   C. fair   D. strict

   5._____

Questions 6-10.

DIRECTIONS: In each of Questions 6 through 10, one word is wrong because it is NOT in keeping with the intended meaning of the statement. First, decide which word is wrongly used; then select as your answer the right word which really belongs in its place.

EXAMPLE

The employee told ill and requested permission to leave early.
  A. felt   B. considered   C. cried   D. spoke

The word "told" is clearly wrong and not in keeping with the intended meaning of the quotation.
The word "felt" (A), however, would clearly convey the intended meaning of the sentence. Option A is correct. Your answer space, therefore, should be marked A.

6. Only unwise supervisors would deliberately overload their subordinates in order to create themselves look good.
  A. delegate   B. make   C. reduce   D. produce

7. In a democratic organization each employee is seen as a special individual kind of fair treatment.
  A. granted   B. denial   C. perhaps   D. deserving

8. In order to function the work flow in an office you should begin by identifying each important procedure being performed in that office.
  A. uniformity   B. study   C. standards   D. reward

9. A wise supervisor tries to save employees' time by simplifying forms or adding forms where possible.
  A. taxing   B. supervising   C. eliminating   D. protecting

10. A public agency, whenever it changes its program, should give requirements to the need for retraining its employees.
  A. legislation   B. consideration
  C. permission   D. advice

Questions 11-15.

DIRECTIONS: Questions 11 through 15 are to be answered ONLY on the basis of the reading passage preceding each question.

11. Things may not always be what they seem to be. Thus, the wise supervisor should analyze his problems and determine whether there is something there that does not meet the eye. For example, what may seem on the surface to be a personality clash between two subordinates may really be a problem of faulty organization, bad communication, or bad scheduling.

3 (#1)

Which one of the following statements BEST supports this passage?
  A. The wise supervisor should avoid personality clashes.
  B. The smart supervisor should figure out what really is going on.
  C. Bad scheduling is the result of faulty organization.
  D. The best supervisor is the one who communicates effectively.

12. Some supervisors, under the pressure of meeting deadlines, become harsh and dictatorial to their subordinates. However, the supervisor most likely to be effective in meeting deadlines is one who absorbs or cushions pressures from above.
According to the passage, if a supervisor wishes to meet deadlines, it is MOST important that he
  A. be informative to his superiors
  B. encourage personal initiative among his subordinates
  C. become harsh and dictatorial to his subordinates
  D. protects his subordinates from pressures from above

13. When giving instructions, a supervisor must always make clear his meaning, leaving no room for misunderstanding. For example, a supervisor who tells a subordinate to do a task "as soon as possible" might legitimately be understood to mean either "it's top priority" or "do it when you can."
Which of the following statements is BEST supported by the passage?
  A. Subordinates will attempt to avoid work by deliberately distorting instructions.
  B. Instructions should be short, since brief instructions are the clearest.
  C. Less educated subordinates are more likely to honestly misunderstand instructions.
  D. A supervisor should give precise instructions that cannot be misinterpreted.

14. Practical formulas are often suggested to simplify what a supervisor should know and how he should behave, such as the four F's (be firm, fair, friendly, and factual). But such simple formulas are really broad principles, not necessarily specific guides in a real situation.
According to the passage, simple formulas for supervisory behavior
  A. are superior to complicated theories and principles
  B. not always of practical use in actual situations
  C. useful only if they are fair and factual
  D. would be better understood if written in clear language

15. Many management decisions are made far removed from the actual place of operations. Therefore, there is a great need for reliable reports and records and, the larger the organization, the greater is the need for such reports and records.
According to the passage, management decisions made far from the place of operations are
  A. dependent to a great extent on reliable reports and records
  B. sometimes in error because of the great distances involved

C. generally unreliable because of poor communications
D. generally more accurate than on-the-scene decisions

16. Assume that you have just been advanced to a supervisory administrative position and have been assigned as supervisor to a new office with subordinates you do not know.
The BEST way for you to establish good relations with these new subordinates would be to
    A. announce that all actions of the previous supervisor are now cancelled
    B. hold a meeting and warn them that you will not tolerate loafing on the job
    C. reassign all your subordinates to new tasks on the theory that a thorough shake-up is good for morale
    D. act fairly and show helpful interest in their work

16._____

17. One of your subordinates asks you to let her arrive at work 15 minutes later than usual but leave for the day 15 minutes later than she usually does. This is temporarily necessary, your subordinate states, because of early morning medication she must give her sick child.
Which of the following would be the MOST appropriate action for you to take?
    A. Suggest to your subordinate that she choose another family doctor
    B. Warn your subordinate that untruthful excuses are not acceptable
    C. Tell your subordinate that you will consider the request and let her know very shortly
    D. Deny the request since late arrival at work interferes with work performance

17._____

18. A young newly-hired employee asked his supervisor several times for advice on private financial matters. The supervisor commented, in a friendly manner, that he considered it undesirable to give such advice.
The supervisor's response was
    A. *unwise*; the supervisor missed an opportunity to advise the employee on an important matter
    B. *wise*; if the financial advice was wrong, it could damage the supervisor's relationship with the subordinate
    C. *unwise*; the subordinate will take up the matter with his fellow workers and probably get poor advice
    D. *wise*; the supervisor should never advise subordinates on any matter

18._____

19. Which of the following is the MOST justified reason for a supervisor to pay any serious attention to a subordinate's off-the-job behavior? The
    A. subordinate's lifestyle is different from the supervisor's way of life
    B. subordinate has become well-known as a serious painter of fine art
    C. subordinate's work has become very poor as a result of his or her personal problems
    D. subordinate is a reserved person who, at work, seldom speaks of personal matters

19._____

20. One of your subordinates complains to you that you assign him to the least pleasant jobs more often than anyone else. You are disturbed by this complaint since you believe you have always rotated such assignments on a fair basis.
    Of the following, it would be BEST for you to tell the complaining subordinate that
    A. you will review your past assignment records and discuss the matter with him further
    B. complaints to supervisors are not the wise way to get ahead on the job
    C. disciplinary action will follow if the complaint is not justified
    D. he may be correct, but you do not have sufficient time to verify the complaint

21. Assume that you have called one of your subordinates into your office to talk about the increasing number of careless errors in her work. Until recently, this subordinate had been doing good work, but this is no longer so. Your subordinate does not seem to respond to your questions about the reason for her poor work.
    In these circumstances, your NEXT step should be to tell her
    A. that her continued silence will result in severe disciplinary action
    B. to request an immediate transfer from your unit
    C. to return when she is ready to respond
    D. to be more open with you so that her work problem can be identified

22. Assume that you are given a complicated assignment with a tight deadline set by your superior. Shortly after you begin work you realize that, if you are to do a top quality job, you cannot possibly meet the deadline.
    In these circumstances, what should be your FIRST course of action?
    A. Continue working as rapidly as possible, hoping that you will meet the deadline after all
    B. Request the assignment be given to an employee whom you believe works faster
    C. Advise your superior of the problem and see whether the deadline can be extended
    D. Advise your superior that the deadline cannot be met and, therefore, you will not start the job

23. Assume that a member of the public comes to you to complain about a long-standing practice of your agency. The complaint seems to be justified.
    Which one of the following is the BEST way for you to handle this situation?
    A. Inform the complainant that you will have the agency practice looked into and that he will be advised of any action taken
    B. Listen politely, express sympathy, and state that you see no fault in the practice
    C. Express agreement with the practice on the ground that it has been in effect for many years
    D. Advise the complainant that things will work out well in good time

24. One of your subordinates tells you that he sees no reason for having departmental safety rules.
 Which one of the following replies would be BEST for you to make?
 A. Rules are meant to be obeyed without question
 B. All types of rules are equally important
 C. Safety rules are meant to protect people from injury
 D. If a person is careful enough, he doesn't have to observe safety rules

25. Assume that a supervisor, when he issues instructions to his subordinates, usually names his superior as the source of these instructions.
 This practice is GENERALLY
 A. *wise*, since if things go wrong, the subordinates will know whom to blame
 B. *unwise*, since it may give the subordinates the impression that the supervisor doesn't really support the instructions
 C. *wise*, since it clearly invites the subordinates to go to higher authority if they don't like the instructions

KEY (CORRECT ANSWERS)

1.	A		11.	B
2.	C		12.	D
3.	D		13.	D
4.	A		14.	B
5.	C		15.	A
6.	B		16.	D
7.	D		17.	C
8.	B		18.	B
9.	C		19.	C
10.	B		20.	A

21. D
22. C
23. A
24. C
25. B

TEST 2

DIRECTIONS: Each question or incomplete statement is followed by several suggested answers or completions. Select the one that BEST answers the question or completes the statement. *PRINT THE LETTER OF THE CORRECT ANSWER IN THE SPACE AT THE RIGHT.*

1. An office aide is assigned as a receptionist in a busy office. The office aide often has stretches of idle time between visitors.
   In this situation, the supervisor should
    A. give the receptionist non-urgent clerical jobs which can quickly be done at the reception desk
    B. offer all office aides an opportunity to volunteer for this assignment
    C. eliminate the receptionist assignment
    D. continue the arrangement unchanged, because receptionist duties are so important nothing should interfere with them

    1.____

2. A supervisor can MOST correctly assume that an employee is not performing up to his usual standard when the employee does not handle a task as skillfully as
    A. do other employees who have received less training
    B. do similar employees having comparable work experience
    C. he has handled it in several recent instances
    D. the supervisor himself could handle it

    2.____

3. Assume that you receive a suggestion that you direct all the typists in a typing pool to complete the identical quantity of work each day.
   For you to adopt this suggestion would be
    A. *advisable*; it will demonstrate the absence of supervisory favoritism
    B *advisable*; all employees in a given title should be treated identically
    C. *inadvisable*; a supervisor should decide on work standards without interference from others
    D. *inadvisable*; it ignores variations in specific assignments and individual skills

    3.____

4. A certain supervisor encouraged her subordinates to tell her if they become aware of possible job problems.
   This practice is good MAINLY because
    A. early awareness of job problems allows more time for seeking solutions
    B. such expected job problems may not develop
    C. the supervisor will be able to solve the job problem without consulting other people
    D. the supervisor will be able to place responsibility for poor work

    4.____

5. Some supervisors will discuss with a subordinate how he is doing on the job only when indicating his mistakes or faults.
   Which of the following is the MOST likely result of such a practice?
    A. The subordinate will become discouraged and frustrated.
    B. Management will set work standards too low.

    5.____

85

C. The subordinate will be favorably impressed by the supervisor's frankness.
D. Supervisors will avoid creating any impression of favoritism.

6. A supervisor calls in a subordinate he supervises to discuss the subordinate's annual work performance, indicating his work deficiencies and also praising his job strengths. The subordinate nods his head as if in agreement with his supervisor's comments on both his strengths and weaknesses, but actually says nothing, even after the supervisor has completed his comments.
At this point, the supervisor should
   A. end the session and assume that the subordinate agrees completely with the evaluation
   B. end the session, since all the subordinate's good and bad points have been identified
   C. ask the supervisor whether the criticism is justified, and, if so, what he, the supervisor, can do to help
   D. thank the subordinate for being so fair-minded in accepting the criticism in a positive manner

7. The successful supervisor is often one who gives serious attention to his subordinates' needs for job satisfaction.
A supervisor who believes this statement is MOST likely to
   A. treat all subordinates in an identical manner, irrespective of individual differences
   B. permit each subordinate to perform his work as he wishes, within reasonable limits
   C. give all subordinates both criticism and praise in equal measure
   D. provide each subordinate with as much direct supervision as possible

8. Assume that you are supervising seven subordinates and have been asked by your superior to prepare an especially complex report due today. Its completion will take the rest of the day. You break down the assignment into simple parts and give a different part to each subordinate.
If you were to explain the work of each subordinate to more than one subordinate, your decision would be
   A. *wise*; this would prevent boredom
   B. *unwise*; valuable time would be lost
   C. *wise*; your subordinates would become well-rounded
   D. *unwise*; your subordinates would lose their competitive spirit

9. Suppose that an office associate whom you supervise has given you a well-researched report on a problem in an area in which he is expert. However, the report lacks solutions or recommendations. You know this office associate to be fearful of stating his opinions.
In these circumstances, you should tell him that
   A. you will seek recommendations on the problem from other, even if less expert, office associates
   B. his work is satisfactory, in hope of arousing him to greater assertiveness

C. you need his advice and expertise, to help you reach a decision on the problem
D. his uncooperative behavior leaves you no choice but to speak to your superior

10. If a supervisor wishes to have the work of his unit completed on schedule, it is usually MOST important to
    A. avoid listening to employees' complaints, thereby discouraging dissatisfaction
    B. perform much of the work himself, since he is generally more capable
    C. observe employees continuously, so they do not slacken their efforts
    D. set up the work carefully, then stay informed as to how it is moving

11. Of the following agencies, the one MOST likely to work out a proposed budget close to its real needs is
    A. a newly-created agency staffed by inexperienced administrators
    B. funded with a considerable amount of money
    C. an existing agency which intends to install new, experimental systems for doing its work
    D. an existing agency which can base its estimate on its experience during the past few years

12. Assume that you are asked to prepare a report on the expected costs and benefits of a proposed new program to be installed in your office. However, you are aware that certain factors are not really measurable in dollars and cents.
    As a result, you should
    A. identify the non-measurable factors and state why they are important
    B. assign a fixed money value to all factors that are not really measurable
    C. recommend that programs containing non-measurable factors should be dropped
    D. assume that the non-measurable factors are really unimportant

13. Assume that you are asked for your opinion as to the necessity for hiring more employees to perform certain revenue-producing work in your office.
    The information that you will MOST likely need in giving an informed opinion is
    A. whether public opinion would favor hiring additional employees
    B. an estimate of the probable additional revenue compared with the additional personnel costs
    C. the total cost of all city operations in contrast to all city revenues
    D. the method by which present employees would be selected for promotion in an expanded operation

14. The MOST reasonable number of subordinate for a supervisor to have is BEST determined by the
    A. average number of subordinates other supervisors have
    B. particular responsibilities given to the supervisor
    C. supervisor's educational background
    D. personalities of the subordinates assigned to the supervisor

15. Most subordinates would need less supervision if they knew what they were supposed to do.
An ESSENTIAL first step in fixing in subordinates' minds exactly what is required of them is to
    A. require that supervisors be firm in their supervision of subordinates
    B. encourage subordinates to determine their own work standards
    C. encourage subordinates to submit suggestions to improve procedures
    D. standardize and simplify procedures and logically schedule activities

16. Assume that you have been asked to recommend an appropriate office layout to correspond with a just completed office reorganization.
Which of the following is it MOST advisable to recommend?
    A. Allocate most of the space for traffic flow
    B. Use the center area only for traffic flow
    C. Situate close to each other those units whose work is closely related
    D. Group in an out-of-the-way corner the supply and file cabinets

17. Although an organization chart will illustrate the formal structure of an agency, it will seldom show a true picture of its actual workings.
Which of the following BEST explains this statement?
Organization charts
    A. are often prepared by employees who may exaggerate their own importance
    B. usually show titles and sometimes names rather than the actual contacts and movements between employees
    C. are likely to discourage the use of official titles, and in so doing promote greater freedom in human relations
    D. usually show the informal arrangements and dealings between employees

18. Assume that a supervisor of a large unit has a variety of tasks to perform, and that he gives each of his subordinates just one set of tasks to do. He never rotates subordinates from one set of tasks to another.
Which one of the following is the MOST likely advantage to be gained by this practice?
    A. Each subordinate will get to know all the tasks of the unit.
    B. The subordinate will be encouraged to learn all they can about all the unit's tasks.
    C. Each subordinate will become an expert in his particular set of tasks.
    D. The subordinates will improve their opportunities for promotion.

19. Listed below are four steps commonly used in trying to solve administrative problems. These four steps are not listed in the order in which they normally would be taken. If they were listed in the proper order, which step should be taken FIRST?
    I. Choosing the most practical solution to the problem
    II. Analyzing the essential facts about the problem
    III. Correctly identifying the problem
    IV. Following up to see if the solution chosen really works

The CORRECT answer is:
A. III   B. I   C. II   D. IV

20. Assume that another agency informally tells you that most of your agency's reports are coming to them with careless errors made by many of your office aides.
    Which one of the following is MOST likely to solve this problem?
    A. Require careful review of all outgoing reports by the supervisors of the office aides
    B. Request the other agency to make necessary corrections whenever such errors come to their attention
    C. Ask the other agency to submit a written report on this situation
    D. Establish a small unit to review all reports received from other agencies

21. Assume that you supervise an office which gets two kinds of work. One kind is high-priority and must be done within two days. The other kind of work must be done within two weeks.
    Which one of the following instructions would be MOST reasonable for you to give to your subordinates in this office?
    A. If a backlog builds up during the day, clean the backlog up first, regardless of priority
    B. Spend half the day doing priority work and the other half doing non-priority work
    C. Generally do the priority work first as soon as it is received
    D. Usually do the work in the order in which it comes in, priority or non-priority

22. An experienced supervisor should do advance planning of his subordinates' work assignments and schedules.
    Which one of the following is the BEST reason for such advance planning?
    It
    A. enables the supervisor to do less supervision
    B. will assure the assignment of varied duties
    C. will make certain a high degree of discipline among subordinates
    D. helps make certain that essential operations are adequately covered

23. Agencies are required to evaluate the performance of their employees.
    Which one of the following would generally be POOR evaluation practice by an agency rater?
    The rater
    A. regularly observes the performance of the employee being rated
    B. in evaluating the employee, acquaints himself with the employee's job
    C. uses objective standards in evaluating the employee being rated
    D. uses different standards in evaluating men and women

24. A good supervisor should have a clear idea of the quantity and quality of his subordinates' work.
Which one of the following sources would normally provide a supervisor with the LEAST reliable information about a subordinate's work performance?
    A. Discussion with a friend of the subordinate
    B. Comments by other supervisors who have worked recently with the subordinate
    C. Opinions of fellow workers who work closely with the subordinate on a daily basis
    D. Comparison with work records of others doing similar work during the same period of time

24.____

25. In order to handle the ordinary work of an office, a supervisor sets up standard work procedures.
The MOST likely benefit of this is to reduce the need to
    A. motivate employees to do superior work
    B. rethink what has to be done every time a routine matter comes up
    C. keep record and write reports
    D. change work procedures as new situations come up

25.____

KEY (CORRECT ANSWERS)

1.	A		11.	D
2.	C		12.	A
3.	D		13.	B
4.	A		14.	B
5.	A		15.	D
6.	C		16.	C
7.	B		17.	B
8.	B		18.	C
9.	C		19.	A
10.	D		20.	A

21.	C
22.	D
23.	D
24.	A
25.	B

EXAMINATION SECTION
TEST 1

DIRECTIONS: Each question or incomplete statement is followed by several suggested answers or completions. Select the one that BEST answers the question or completes the statement. *PRINT THE LETTER OF THE CORRECT ANSWER IN THE SPACE AT THE RIGHT.*

1. The BEST technique for a superintendent to use to gain and keep the respect of his subordinates is to

    A. approve and commend all work done
    B. be scrupulously fair in dealing with all subordinates
    C. offer specific criticism at each phase of each job
    D. use contests to motivate speed up of work

2. The MOST important of the following qualities for a good superintendent to have is

    A. a dignified appearance to set a standard for his men to follow
    B. neatness of dress so that his subordinates will have a model to follow if promoted
    C. the ability to handle men
    D. skill in writing reports which are to be forwarded to higher echelons

3. In making decisions, a new superintendent who wishes to impress his subordinates should make these decisions

    A. after consulting his subordinates for their ideas
    B. as rapidly as possible, changing them if they are wrong
    C. only after studying all the information related to the matter
    D. promptly and stick to them even if an error is made

4. After a superintendent has submitted his service ratings of the work of his subordinates, one of them whose work has not been satisfactory complains to the superintendent that his rating was unjustified.
For the superintendent to avoid discussing the rating but to point out two or three specific instances where the employee's work is below standard is

    A. *desirable;* an employee should be told what parts of his work are unsatisfactory
    B. *undesirable;* once a rating has been submitted, there is no point in discussing it
    C. *desirable;* entering into a general argument is bad for the discipline of the department
    D. *undesirable;* it would have been better to have explained how the rating was arrived at

5. A new employee who has shown himself capable of doing superior work during the first month of his probationary period falls below this standard during the second month. For the supervisor to wait until the end of the probationary period and then recommend that the man be dropped if his work is still unsatisfactory is

    A. *undesirable;* he should have been discharged when his work became unsatisfactory
    B. *desirable;* there is no place in the department for unsatisfactory employees
    C. *undesirable;* the supervisor should immediately attempt to determine the cause of the unsatisfactory performance
    D. *desirable;* the employee is entitled to a chance to prove himself

6. The one which is NOT a principle of leadership is:

    A. Know your job, yourself, and your men
    B. Be sure that a task is understood, supervised, and accomplished
    C. See responsibility and develop a sense of responsibility in your men
    D. Use every effort to shift responsibility to lower echelons

7. A superintendent starting a safety campaign should be aware that

    A. accidents are more likely to occur to the same few people in an organization
    B. accidents occur equally to all kinds of people
    C. people who worry are usually more careful and, therefore, have a lower accident rate
    D. the physical and emotional condition of a person has no effect on his accident potential

8. At a staff meeting of foremen, it was said, *The most important job you foremen have is to get across to your subordinates the desirability of achieving our department's goals and the importance of the jobs they are performing toward reaching our objectives.*
The adoption of this point of view would tend to create a department

    A. in which less supervision is required of the work of the average employee
    B. having more clearly defined lines of authority
    C. in which most employees would be capable of taking over a supervisory position when necessary
    D. in which supervisors would tend to neglect their primary mission of getting the assigned work completed efficiently

9. A comment made by an employee about a training course was, *We never know how we are getting along in that course.* The error in training methods to which such a criticism points is

    A. insufficient participation by the students in the course
    B. failure to develop a feeling of need for the material being presented in the class
    C. no attempt is being made to connect the new material being presented with what is presently in use in a department
    D. no goals have been set for the students participating

10. When a superintendent first assumes command of an area, which one of the following tasks should have the LOWEST priority?

    A. Making an effort to meet and know his men
    B. Ascertaining the problem areas
    C. Developing a good rapport with his subordinate officers
    D. Studying the organization of his area with a view to specific reorganization

11. Which of the following steps would be BEST for a superintendent to take if he is to obtain maximum gains in the productivity of his group?

    A. Formulate a specific plan that is complete and relatively inflexible
    B. Leave his own program fairly open but plan for the most effective use of his manpower
    C. Study all of the factors in the work situation and arrange them in order of priority
    D. Consider the solution to problems only when they occur

12. Assume that, as superintendent, your policy is to consult your subordinates for assistance in formulating decisions, when feasible.
    Of the following, the benefit MOST likely to result from this policy is that

    A. your subordinates will become more knowledgeable in other aspects of the work
    B. your decisions will have greater acceptance than when made alone
    C. there will be more *right* decisions made
    D. your workload will be considerably lessened

13. Assume that you are a newly-appointed superintendent, and a report has been submitted to you by one of your foremen, which contains an extensive amount of daily productivity data. On the basis of your knowledge, you seriously question some of the data.
    Which of the following actions would probably be MOST advisable for you to take FIRST?

    A. Accept the report since the foreman has apparently done extensive work to obtain the data
    B. Request that copies of the source material for the report be given to you
    C. Return the report to the foreman for his signature
    D. Question the veracity of the writer

14. Assume that one of your foremen, who is otherwise capable, consistently submits badly written reports.
    To improve his ability to write reports, it would be MOST advisable to

    A. carefully go over his reports with him, indicating their weaknesses and making suggestions for improvement
    B. provide him with some textbooks on report writing and give him a deadline to complete reading them
    C. insist that each report be rewritten until it is acceptable
    D. have another foreman collaborate with him in writing his reports

15. Assume that, as superintendent, you have been requested to write a lengthy report for your supervisor. You decide to include a summary of the report and its findings.
    The summary should be useful MAINLY because

    A. it will pinpoint your conclusions and recommendations
    B. it probably includes as much as the rest of the report
    C. the subject of the report is probably routine in nature
    D. the summary may include material not mentioned previously

16. When a superintendent finds it necessary to let a man know that he is dissatisfied with his level of performance, which of the following tactics would *usually* prove MOST effective in improving his performance?

    A. The superintendent should *chew the man out* in order to prevent the mistakes from recurring.
    B. Once criticism has been made, the superintendent should be sure to continuously remind the man of the seriousness of the mistakes.
    C. When making his criticism, the superintendent should guard against referring to any work that was well done since this would reduce the effect of his criticism.
    D. The superintendent should focus his criticism on the mistakes being made and should avoid downgrading the subordinate personally.

17. While training a group of new men, a superintendent notices that one of them is not paying attention.
Of the following, the MOST appropriate method for the superintendent to use in order to properly sustain attention and maintain discipline would *generally* be for him to

    A. reprimand the new man immediately in front of the group
    B. call a break period and then privately find out why this man is not paying attention
    C. ask the man to leave the training area until he has a chance to speak to him
    D. ignore the man's behavior since the man will be the one who will suffer later on

18. Several weeks after you begin your job as superintendent, you realize that although your working days seem busy, you are not accomplishing as much as you would like.
Of the following, the BEST solution to your problem would be to

    A. figure out how much time you spend on various activities and, from this, adjust your time schedule as needed
    B. accept the fact that you were not ready for the promotion and request that you be placed in your former position
    C. realize that there is a limit to how much any man can accomplish and be satisfied with what you already do
    D. eliminate the routine paperwork to allow time for more pressing work

19. One factor which may be considered in determining the best span of control for a supervisor over his immediate subordinates is the position of the supervisor in the structure of the organization.
It is usually considered MOST desirable that the number of subordinates immediately supervised by a higher echelon supervisor _____ the number supervised by lower level supervisors.

    A. have no relation at all to
    B. be roughly the same as
    C. be larger than
    D. be smaller than

20. Suppose that a superintendent wishes to hold a subordinate strictly accountable for carrying out an order.
Of the following, the BEST course of action for the superintendent to adopt is to

    A. be sure that at least one other officer is present when the order is given to the subordinate
    B. give the order, explain the order, and have the subordinate repeat the order to be sure there is no misunderstanding
    C. issue a direct and complete order in writing to the subordinate
    D. tell the subordinate what is to be done and then relate the job to be done to appropriate department regulations

21. Proper planning of his work by a superintendent will NOT generally result in the

    A. apportionment of time to each aspect of his job in accord with its relative importance
    B. delegation of fewer tasks to subordinates
    C. determination of the best way of doing a job
    D. handling of all details involved in coordinating his work with a minimum of effort

22. Suppose that one of the clerks in your office discovers what appears to be an incorrect figure on a weekly statistical report submitted by one of the sections in your control.
The MOST appropriate action for you as a superintendent to take is to

   A. tell the clerk to use his best judgment and insert what he believes is the correct figure
   B. return the report to the section with a memo stating that the report is incorrect
   C. call the foreman of the section and ask him to check the accuracy of the questionable figure
   D. send your clerk to the section and have him double-check the original data with the section clerk

23. A superintendent observes that reports reaching him from foremen and assistant foremen tend to emphasize the favorable and play down the unfavorable aspects of conditions existing in the sections.
The MOST valid conclusion to draw from this, of the following, is that the

   A. subordinates are influenced by a normal tendency to put themselves and their work in the best light
   B. subordinates are willing to take a chance that their somewhat optimistic reports will not be checked too carefully
   C. superintendent has been, perhaps subconsciously, indirectly suggesting to his subordinates that he would prefer to receive good, rather than bad, news
   D. superintendent has been motivated to accept such reports since he is interested more in getting work done than in getting meticulous reports

24. If a superintendent realizes that his foremen frequently write reports which require considerable revision before they can be forwarded, the superintendent would BEST improve future reports prepared by these foremen by

   A. assigning a skilled officer to rewrite these reports
   B. discussing with the foremen needed revisions in their reports
   C. emphasizing the importance of reports and report writing
   D. sending back the worst reports for rewriting without comment, thus letting the officers learn by doing

25. Many reports are sent to the office of a superintendent conveying information about the performance of the men and equipment in the section.
The BEST reason for the superintendent to regularly analyze the information in these reports is to

   A. discover the sections which are not meeting departmental work standards
   B. account for the time he is required to spend in direct field supervision of his force
   C. establish objective measures for disciplinary action
   D. help him train his subordinate supervisors to establish better non-official relationships with the men

26. A superintendent at his first meeting with a new foreman senses an attitude of hostility. Of the following, it would be BEST for him to

   A. firmly assert his authority in order to nip a potentially troublesome situation in the bud
   B. make a quick check with this foreman's previous superintendent to *get a line* on the man
   C. say nothing at this time about the foreman's attitude but try to learn the reasons for it if it continues
   D. tell the foreman that he finds his attitude very unreasonable

27. In delegating authority to a foreman, a superintendent should ORDINARILY

   A. define the limits of the delegated authority as precisely and as specifically as possible
   B. evaluate the *effectiveness potential* of the foreman to determine whether or not to set predetermined limits
   C. make no attempt to define the limits of such authority until the foreman himself discovers from practical experience what the limits should be
   D. depend on the temperament of the foreman to set his own reasonable limits

28. A serious error has been discovered by a senior superintendent in work done under your supervision as a superintendent.
Your BEST response would be:

   A. *I am very sorry but you must admit I cannot check every detail of this complex job.*
   B. *I am sorry it happened, and I'm really surprised that Foreman Smith would make such a mistake.*
   C. *I'll look into it and do all I can to prevent a recurrence.*
   D. *No matter what I tell these officers, they don't get it. We need a real training program.*

29. As a result of examination, you receive an appointment as superintendent.
Of the following, the FIRST thing you should do is to

   A. analyze the duties and responsibilities of your new position
   B. carefully observe the procedures of experienced superintendents
   C. develop your skills in human relations
   D. read recognized texts on specific practices in your area

30. The PRINCIPAL argument in favor of filling top positions in the department by promotion rather than by open competitive examinations is that this procedure

   A. assures that candidates will be given due credit for experience
   B. assures that capable men will get the jobs
   C. encourages a career service within the department
   D. increases public interest in the examination

KEY (CORRECT ANSWERS)

1.	B	16.	D
2.	C	17.	B
3.	C	18.	A
4.	D	19.	D
5.	C	20.	C
6.	D	21.	B
7.	A	22.	C
8.	A	23.	A
9.	D	24.	B
10.	D	25.	A
11.	C	26.	C
12.	B	27.	A
13.	B	28.	C
14.	A	29.	A
15.	A	30.	C

TEST 2

DIRECTIONS: Each question or incomplete statement is followed by several suggested answers or completions. Select the one that BEST answers the question or completes the statement. *PRINT THE LETTER OF THE CORRECT ANSWER IN THE SPACE AT THE RIGHT.*

1. The MOST important factor in the success of the department training program is

   A. adequate training center facilities
   B. an adequate supply of study material on department practices
   C. coordination with training programs of other large related departments
   D. officers who know common procedures and can instruct men

   1.___

2. The more complex an organization and the more highly specialized the division of work, the GREATER the need for

   A. coordinating authority
   B. clearer division of supervisory responsibility
   C. performance standards
   D. strict discipline

   2.___

3. The MOST important of the following factors for a superintendent to consider when setting up a work schedule for a job modification is the

   A. cost of manpower to perform the job
   B. availability of men and helpers to do the job
   C. cost of the equipment that will be used on this job
   D. quality of the equipment that will be used on this job

   3.___

4. A supervisor requests his foreman to submit a written report to him by a certain date. After starting work on this assignment, the foreman determines that he cannot meet the deadline if he is to do a complete and thorough job on this report.
   In this case, the foreman should

   A. inform his supervisor of the situation
   B. work to the deadline and then ask for an extension
   C. meet the deadline even if he has to submit an inadequate report
   D. ask another foreman for assistance

   4.___

5. Of the following, the BEST way to begin criticism of a report written by a subordinate is:

   A. If you keep on like this, you'll never learn how to write
   B. This is partly right; now take it back and fix it up
   C. This is pretty good, but I think we can improve it
   D. You know you can do better than this

   5.___

6. A superintendent is called upon to administer an order with which he does not agree. He has reason to believe his men do not agree with it either.
   In discussing the order with them, he should express

   A. his belief that the order will undoubtedly be changed later
   B. such reasons as he may know that support the order
   C. that he has unsuccessfully taken the matter up with his superiors
   D. that he is basically in accord with their disapproval of the order

   6.___

7. One of the factors making it difficult for officers to introduce new methods which will alter procedures that have been in existence for some time is the tendency of people to

    A. change likes and dislikes rapidly
    B. dislike change
    C. dislike experts
    D. like old ideas because they are old

8. In comparison with the number of men under a supervisor in other agencies, the number of men under a superintendent might seem excessive.
However, a factor which makes such conclusion ERRONEOUS is the

    A. command nature of the superintendent's authority
    B. large amount of authority delegated to the superintendent
    C. small number of men under his supervisor to whom the superintendent reports
    D. uniformity of the work supervised by the superintendent

9. The need in departmental administration is for foremen to project their thinking to a higher level, for superintendents to see the problems of the department.
This statement describes the need for employees who

    A. consider their jobs as inferior to those of a higher level
    B. plan operations on a broader basis than their own districts
    C. understand their jobs as part of the larger job of the department
    D. do their jobs as well as they possibly can

10. The one of the following which is NOT a sound procedure for a superintendent to follow is to

    A. create a feeling of warmth between himself and his men
    B. ignore petty grievances until they work themselves out
    C. instill confidence and security among subordinates
    D. take prompt action on a decision once it is made

11. Which of the following acts by a superintendent would be MOST subject to criticism on the basis of principles underlying good supervision?
He

    A. allows a man who has shown a talent for such things a large measure of initiative in devising new methods of doing the work
    B. asks his men to give him their opinions as to methods of doing the work but, in some cases, does not accept these opinions as a basis for change
    C. gives no definite answer on being told by one man of his difficulties in working with another but tells him he will look into the matter
    D. tries to avoid disappointing either side by giving an answer that is not decisive but to some extent satisfactory to both, when asked to settle a matter by men who differ as to a proper procedure

12. Use of competition between squads or gangs in an accident-reduction program is

    A. *desirable;* it gives men an incentive
    B. *desirable;* all have an opportunity
    C. *undesirable;* it may arouse ill-feeling
    D. *undesirable;* prizes are expensive

13. With respect to delegation of authority, a superintendent should be guided by the principle that he should

    A. delegate as much authority as he effectively can
    B. discourage his men from consulting him on section matters
    C. keep all authority centralized in himself
    D. personally confirm all decisions made by his men

14. A superintendent is faced with the problem of a conflict in authority between two foremen.
    The FINAL step he should take in handling this problem is to

    A. consider the effect his orders will have on the subordinates
    B. find out what rules have been applied to similar situations
    C. issue the orders which designate the action to be taken
    D. point out to the foremen the importance of harmonious working relationships

15. In explaining new work procedures to his foremen, a superintendent should place LEAST emphasis on

    A. how the new procedures are to be carried out
    B. what is to be accomplished by the new procedures
    C. when the new procedures are to be started
    D. who ordered the change to the new procedures

16. A supervisor asks his superintendent for a report on the capabilities of a new piece of equipment. The superintendent asks a foreman to turn in the report; and the foreman, in turn, assigns the job to an assistant foreman. The assistant foreman makes the investigation and writes the report. The report goes up through channels to the supervisor and turns out to be full of inaccuracies.
    Who is to be held responsible for the inaccurate report?
    The

    A. assistant foreman *only*
    B. superintendent *only*
    C. foreman and assistant foreman *only*
    D. superintendent, foreman, and assistant foreman

17. The one of the following which is MOST likely to have the MOST lasting good effect on a man's morale is

    A. a good social and recreational program
    B. a suggestion system with cash awards for good ideas
    C. liberal rest periods and coffee breaks
    D. recognition by his superiors of his efforts

18. Suppose your supervisor tells you he is contemplating a certain assignment for one of your section foremen. You consider this a wrong assignment for a good man.
    You should

    A. say nothing since this is a matter to be handled by your superior
    B. speak to the foreman advising him to refuse the assignment
    C. suggest the assignment of another foreman fitted for the job
    D. tell the supervisor you can't spare this man

19. In rating a man's work, a superintendent should be MOST aware that

    A. a man's home environment should be taken into consideration when this has affected the quality of his work
    B. a man's rating should not be influenced by his previous rating
    C. a new man should be rated on the same basis as senior employees
    D. the job classification grade of the man should not be considered

20. The one of the following which is an ADVANTAGE of the employee service rating system is that

    A. an above-average rating will bring the employee an added increment
    B. employees receive formal notification of their rating immediately after the end of the rating year
    C. evaluation of supervisors' ratings by department personnel boards contributes to application of more uniform rating standards
    D. ratings are assigned on a proportional basis which insures that not too many higher ratings are given out

21. In a section, there are usually some assignments that are disliked by the men. To assign men to these jobs as a disciplinary measure after a rule violation is UNDESIRABLE because

    A. severity of the punishment should be related to the seriousness of the offense, such assignments being reserved for the most serious offenses
    B. such assignments should be based on more valid factors such as the requirements of the job and the needs and abilities of the men
    C. the men assigned are sure to do a poor job
    D. the number of violations exceeds the number of such assignments, resulting in inequity

22. Department policy with respect to permitting men to receive presents from private citizens on their routes should be

    A. not to allow it
    B. to allow it at Christmas
    C. to allow if if other city departments follow the practice
    D. to allow if it the superintendent authorizes it

23. As an organizational unit of the department, the function of the sanitary education unit is BEST described as

    A. coordinating   B. housekeeping   C. preventative   D. regulatory

24. The employees' suggestion award program, in addition to bringing forth new ideas, is of MOST value to the department in terms of

    A. developing a competitive spirit among employees and groups
    B. fostering in individual employees a sense of participation
    C. giving an objective basis for employee evaluation and training
    D. keeping lower level supervisors alert and *on their toes*

25. A survey in the sanitation department showed for the first time that a substantial number of streets previously classified as *fair* were now classified as *dirty*.
    The LEAST probable reason for this change is the

    A. abundance of heavy litter
    B. shifts in population
    C. very hot summer
    D. winter of heavy snow

26. Leadership is the ability to act in a manner designed to secure cooperation on behalf of an established purpose. Which one of the following indicates that a superintendent is exercising leadership in the manner defined here?

    A. He delegates full authority and responsibility to his foremen to settle grievances at the section level.
    B. He explains to his subordinates the reasons for any changes in established procedures.
    C. He gives none of the men in his command a below-standard performance evaluation.
    D. His area has the lowest accident rate in the borough.

27. Of the following, the MAIN goal of a superintendent in a safety program should be to

    A. stress safety as an important factor in producing more work
    B. make department employees recognize the physical hazards of the job
    C. lessen the dissatisfaction of older employees with what they consider to be restrictive safety practices
    D. produce a safety-conscious work environment in which the men themselves try to achieve safer work methods

28. For a superintendent to permit his subordinates to participate in making decisions is usually desirable, when practicable, MAINLY because

    A. better decisions may be arrived at
    B. it will eliminate grievances in the long run
    C. subordinates acquire more prestige as a result of participating in decision making
    D. such decisions become virtually self-executing

29. A newly-appointed superintendent made a special effort to learn the names of all the officers and men in his command and to address them by name whenever possible.
    GENERALLY speaking, such a procedure is considered

    A. *good;* since people like to feel they are being thought of as individuals
    B. *poor;* since the men are apt to feel they will be under excessive supervision
    C. *good;* since the officers and men will realize that exceptionally good work will be recognized and rewarded
    D. *poor;* since the subordinates will suspect ulterior motives are influencing the superintendent

30. The principle of administration that the responsibility of higher officers for the acts of subordinates MUST be absolute means that
    A. discretionary authority should not be delegated
    B. each and every subordinate bears the fullest measure of self-responsibility and self-control
    C. each superior officer is held responsible for the acts of his subordinates
    D. officers at the same echelon in the organization cannot escape responsibility for each other's acts

KEY (CORRECT ANSWERS)

1.	D	16.	D
2.	A	17.	D
3.	B	18.	C
4.	A	19.	B
5.	C	20.	C
6.	B	21.	B
7.	B	22.	A
8.	D	23.	C
9.	C	24.	B
10.	B	25.	A
11.	D	26.	B
12.	A	27.	D
13.	A	28.	A
14.	C	29.	A
15.	D	30.	C

BASIC FUNDAMENTALS OF WATER QUALITY

TABLE OF CONTENTS

	Page
Reasons for Water Treatment	1
Quality Control Tests	2
Drinking Water Standards	3
Composition of Water from Various Sources	5
Self-Purification and Storage	8
Methods of Water Treatment	10

BASIC FUNDAMENTALS OF WATER QUALITY

Water, if strictly defined in the chemical sense, is H_2O a compound which, like all other pure substances, has a definite and constant composition. Therefore it should, like any pure compound, exhibit predictable chemical and physical characteristics. Indeed, the properties of a pure compound are so dependable that they may be used for identification if an unknown sample is submitted to a laboratory. In other words, water might be expected to be the same, regardless of its origin. In this context, discussing the "quality" of water, or of water from a particular source, would be rather meaningless.

One of the predictable physical properties of this widely distributed compound is a rather remarkable power to dissovle other materials. Familiar as we are with its characteristics, we tend to accept the solvent power of water as a matter of course, and to see nothing remarkable in it. But if water is compared with other known liquids, it is found that none of the others is capable of dissolving so wide a range of compounds of varying compositions. As a result, water seldom if very occurs in nature in a chemically pure state.

In addition to a variety of dissolved materials, water drawn from a natural source usually contains particles of insoluble, or at least undissolved, materials in suspension. The size and the concentration of these suspended particles vary considerably, depending upon the source, from the sand grains sometimes present in rapid, turbulent surface streams to the submicroscopic dispersions known as colloids. Included among the suspended particles, there may be living cells of thousands of different kinds of microorganisms.

Thus, when we speak of the quality of water, our concern is not really with the water itself, but with the other materials present. It is these impurities which determine, to a very large degree, the suitability of a water source for human uses, the problems associated with utilizing it, and the kind and extent of treatment required.

Reasons for Water Treatment

In the broadest possible terms, the objectives of water treatment may be classified under three general headings: (1) to protect the health of the community, (2) to supply a product which is esthetically desirable, and (3) to protect the property of the consumers. Each of these is so broad that it requires further explanation, and each embraces several specific methods of treatment.

Protection of the public health implies first that the treated water must be free of microorganisms capable of causing human disease, and second that the concentrations of any chemical substances which are poisonous or otherwise harmful must be reduced to safe levels. Only rarely do raw water supplies contain significant levels of toxic chemicals. But, more often than not, the microbiological quality of the water requires improvement or protection. In the United States, this aspect of water treatment has progressed to the point that the physiological safety of public water supplies usually is taken for granted. In some parts of the world, it is considered necessary when visiting a strange city to carry a private supply of drinking water, or to inquire whether it is safe to drink the local supply. The situation in the United States, which is unquestionably a credit to the water treatment profession, has permitted increased attention to the other two general objectives mentioned in the previous paragraph.

An esthetically desirable water supply requires that the final product shall be as low as possible in color, turbidity, and suspended solids, as cold as possible, and free from undesirable tastes and odors. Since the subject of tastes and odors is highly subjective, it may be impossible to produce a product which is equally pleasing to all consumers. However, strong, distinctive tastes and odors, as well as those which are disagreeable to a significant percentage of the population, are definitely to be avoided. The esthetic quality of a water supply cannot be completely divorced from the question of public health, since objections to the taste, odor, color, etc. of a perfectly safe public supply may prompt consumers to use water from another source which is more attractive, but which, due to lack of protection, may be considerably more dangerous.

The question of property protection is a broad one, and its specific implications depend upon the purpose for which the water is used. Thus the requirements may, and occasionally do, vary among different consumers using the same supply. For domestic supplies, the usual requirements are that the water shall not be excessively corrosive to plumbing and other metal equipment, that it shall not deposit troublesome quantities of scale, and that it shall not stain porcelain plumbing fixtures. For industrial purposes, the requirements may be even more stringent. For example, more than 10 ppm of chlorides interfere with the manufacture of insulating paper. Generally speaking, public suppliers do not find it practical to meet the strict and sometimes varied requirements of their industrial customers. Instead, they maintain a quality suitable for domestic consumption, and if necessary the industries provide further treatment on their own premises.

Quality Control Tests

In his efforts to maintain the quality of his product, the operator or superintendent of a water treatment plant relies upon various chemical and physical tests. In this way, he accomplishes several purposes. Most importantly, perhaps, he assures himself of his success in meeting the standards which are required and desired. If for any reason the quality temporarily becomes unsatisfactory, the test results advise him of the problem, and permit prompt corrective action. By keeping permanent records of the results, he is in a position to demonstrate the quality of his product to the regulatory authorities, or to any other interested individual or agency.

Tests used for monitoring or controlling water quality are suggested by the objectives listed in the previous section. Few, if any, plants find it necessary to perform all the tests discussed in this manual. Ordinarily, the only tests selected for frequent, regular performance are those pertinent to the quality problems experienced at a particular plant. Other tests may be run less frequently to periodically provide a more complete evaluation of the water quality. Samples of the raw water as well as the treated water are often analyzed, since the former may provide information which is necessary to the control of the treatment plant. In some types of treatment, it is desirable in addition to analyze samples collected at intermediate points. Many suppliers also find it advisable to test samples collected from various parts of the distribution system to assure that the water quality is as acceptable when it reaches the consumer as when it leaves the treatment plant.

Determinations of bacteriological quality are most often based upon measurements of the numbers of "coliform bacteria." Although this group of organisms is not known to cause human disease directly, its presence and survival is considered to indicate the potential presence of disease organisms (pathogens), and consequently the number of coliforms present is strictly regulated. In some plants, the enumeration of coliforms is supplemented by the "total plate count," which is an approximate measurement of the total microbial population of the water, or by determining the numbers of one particular species of the coliform group, *Escherichia coli*.

In the vast majority of plants, especially in the United States, control of the bacteriological quality of the water is accomplished by means of chlorination. Therefore, the determination of residual chlorine in its various forms becomes a most important analysis, even though it may not be rigorously correct to consider it a direct means of monitoring the water quality. Closely related to the measurement of residual chlorine is the determination of chlorine demand, which is currently defined as the difference between the concentration of chlorine added and the concentration remaining after a specified period of time. Measurement of the chlorine demand of the raw water is often essential to successful control of the bacteriological quality of the finished product, particularly if the chlorine demand of the source tends to be variable.

Tests for chemical substances known to be poisonous are not ordinarily conducted routinely unless there is reason to suspect the presence of one or more such materials. If the previous history of the water supply, or other circumstance, indicates the possibility of a problem of this kind, the analytical program should include measurement of the concentration of the offending substance, probably both before and after treatment. Otherwise, tests of this type might be included among those which are performed only periodically.

Among the tests related to the esthetic quality of the water, determinations of color, turbidity, suspended solids, and temperature are important. The measurement of taste and odor, unfortunately, is almost as subjective in the laboratory as in the consumer's home or place of business, notwithstanding various attempts to improve its quantitative aspects. For this reason, some plants, in which taste and odor problems are rare, seldom if ever perform the determinations routinely, but rely upon complaints to advise them of the occurrence of a problem. In other places, less fortunate, where strong or disagreeable tastes and odors are a frequent problem, such tests may be a regular part of the quality control program. In a few instances, specific substances such as sulfides and phenols, which are known to affect taste and odor may be measured. Likewise, the determination of iron and manganese may be included in this group, because excessive quantities of either may affect both taste and color. The measurement of dissolved oxygen is sometimes included too, since the majority of people seem to prefer the flavor of water in which the oxygen content is near saturation.

For domestic purposes, the analyses related to protection of property include those which reveal the tendency of the water to corrode metals or to deposit scale. The important tests in this group are those for pH, acidity, alkalinity, total hardness, and calcium. Sometimes a determination of conductivity and total solids may be included, and under certain circumstances a measurement of the concentration of sulfates is important.

Drinking Water Standards

The U. S. Department of Health, Education, and Welfare, through its agency, the U. S. Public Health Service, has published revised standards for the quality of drinking water. Although the federal Public Health Regulations govern only interstate carriers and certain other specified installations, their standards are widely used as guide by other regulatory agencies. Many of the latter have incorporated the PHS standards wholly or in part into their own rules.

Some of the provisions of the Public Health Service standards are summarized below. It must be noted, however, that the complete report[1] from which this information is abstracted includes a great deal of supplementary material which is important in the interpretation and application of the standards. Therefore, the figures quoted do not apply strictly nor without qualification in all cases.

The standard of bacteriological quality is based upon the number of coliform bacteria present. Detailed sampling and testing procedures are specified, and a complete and fairly elaborate description of the method of evaluation sets forth precisely what results are required of an acceptable supply. In effect, the number of coliform bacteria is limited to not more than one organism per 100 ml of water on the average, with not more than five per cent of the samples tested showing numbers greater than this limit.

In regard to physical properties, the turbidity should be less than five units, the color less than 15 units, and the threshold odor number less than three. If the turbidity standard is satisfied, the suspended solids will not be detectable.

"Recommended" limits of concentration established for a number of chemical substances appear in Table VII. These are not absolute standards. Rather it is suggested that these materials "should not be present in a water supply in excess of the listed concentrations where . . . other more suitable supplies are or can be made available."

TABLE I
RECOMMENDED CONCENTRATION LIMITS

Substance	Maximum Concentration, mg/l
Alkyl Benzene Sulfonate	0.5
Arsenic	0.01
Chloride	250.
Copper	1.
Carbon Chloroform Extract	0.2
Cyanide	0.01
Fluoride	0.8-1.7 (See PHS Standards)
Iron	0.3
Manganese	0.05
Nitrate	45.
Phenols	0.001
Sulfate	250.
Total Dissolved Solids	500.
Zinc	5.

In addition to the recommended standards which appear in Table I, concentration limits for certain constituents are established which may be considered absolute, in that exceding any one of the limits listed provides grounds for rejecting the supply. These figures appear in Table II.

TABLE II
ABSOLUTE CONCENTRATION LIMITS

Substance	Maximum Concentration, mg/l
Arsenic	0.05
Barium	1.0
Cadmium	0.01
Chromium, Hexavalent	0.05
Cyanide	0.2
Fluoride	See Text
Lead	0.05
Selenium	0.01
Silver	0.05

For Fluoride, both the recommended and absolute limits are related to the climate of the locality in question. For the greatest part of New York State, the recommended optimum is 1.1 mg/l, the recommended upper limit is 1.5 mg/l and the absolute limit is 2.2 mg/l. For a small area in the northern part of the state, the corresponding limits are 1.2, 1.7 and 2.4 mg/l, and in the extreme southeastern part, 1.0, 1.3 and 2.0 mg/l.

Radioactivity is also limited, but the acceptability of a given supply is dependent to some extent upon exposure from other sources. A water supply is unconditionally acceptable in this respect if the content of Radium 226 is less than three micro-micro-curies per liter, the content of Strontium 90 is less than 10 micro-micro-curies per liter, and the gross beta-ray activity is less than one microcurie per liter. If the radioactivity of the water supply exceeds the values stated, then its acceptability is judged on the basis of consideration of other sources of radioactivity in the environment.

Composition of Water from Various Sources

As suggested before, virtually all the water used to supply human requirements has at some time, usually quite recently, fallen to the surface of the earth as rain or some other form of precipitation. At this stage, the quantity of foreign material it contains is likely to be at a minimum. Nevertheless, even rain water is not chemically pure H_2O. Not only does it dissolve the gases of the atmosphere as it falls, but it also collects dust and other solid materials suspended in the air. Since the atmospheric solids depend upon both the composition of the soil below and the materials released into the air from combustion, industrial processes, and other sources, analyses of rain or other forms of precipitation reveal surprising variations. In general, however, rainwater may be expected to be very soft, to be low in total solids and alkalinity, to have a pH value somewhat below neutrality, and to be quite corrosive to many metals. A "typical" analysis, subject to the variations mentioned above, might appear as follows:

Constituent	Value	Units
Hardness	19	mg/l as $CaCO_3$
Calcium	16	mg/l as $CaCO_3$
Magnesium	3	mg/l as $CaCO_3$
Sodium	6	mg/l as Na
Ammonium	0.8	mg/l as N
Bicarbonate	12	mg/l as $CaCO_3$
Acidity	4	mg/l as $CaCO_3$
Chloride	9	mg/l as Cl
Sulfate	10	mg/l as SO_4
Nitrate	0.1	mg/l as N
pH	6.8	

After the water reaches the surface of the ground, it passes over soil and rock into lakes, streams, and reservoirs, or it percolates through the soil and rock into the ground water. In the process, a great variety of materials may be dissolved or taken into suspension. Consequently, it may be expected that the composition of both the surface waters and the ground water of a given area reflects the geology of the region, that is, the composition of the underlying rock formations and of the soils derived from them. In general, the presence of readily soluble formations near the surface, such as gypsum, rock salt, or the various forms of limestone, produce relatively marked effects upon the waters of the area. On the other hand, in the presence of less soluble formations, such as sandstone or granite, the composition of the water tends to remain more like that of rain. As one might expect, local variations are often considerable and occasionally extreme, both in the concentration of any one constituent and in the proportions of the various materials present. The examples given below should be considered with this in view. They are typical only in that they are not remarkable.

Surface water, in an area in which limestone is an important constituent of the geologic formations, might have a composition similar to the following:

Hardness	120	mg/l as $CaCO_3$
Calcium	80	mg/l as $CaCO_3$
Magnesium	40	mg/l as $CaCO_3$
Sodium & Potassium	19	mg/l as Na
Bicarbonate	106	mg/l as $CaCO_3$
Chloride	23	mg/l as Cl
Sulfate	38	mg/l as SO_4
Nitrate	0.4	mg/l as N
Iron	0.3	mg/l as Fe
Silica	18	mg/l as SiO_2
Carbon Dioxide	4	mg/l as $CaCO_3$
pH	7.8	

In such an area, the ground water often contains more hardness and bicarbonate than the surface waters. This is due in part to the longer period of contact with soil and rock, and in part to the fact that carbon dioxide, contributed by the decomposition of organic matter in the soil, greatly increases the solubility of some of the constituents. The folowing analysis might be considered typical of well or spring water in a limestone area:

Hardness	201	mg/l as $CaCO_3$
Calcium	142	mg/l as $CaCO_3$
Magnesium	59	mg/l as $CaCO_3$
Sodium & Potassium	20	mg/l as Na
Bicarbonate	143	mg/l as $CaCO_3$
Chloride	23	mg/l as Cl
Sulfate	59	mg/l as SO_4
Nitrate	0.06	mg/l as N
Iron	0.18	mg/l as Fe
Silica	12	mg/l as SiO_2
Carbon Dioxide	14	mg/l as $CaCO_3$
pH	7.4	

In areas in which the underlying formations are insoluble, that is, where they consist of sand, sandstone, clay, shale, or igneous rocks, the waters tend to he softer and more acid. In general, their content of most dissolved materials is lower. Acidity, however, may be higher than in hard water areas, since carbon dioxide picked up from the soil is not neutralized. Excepting in some areas of igneous rock, iron also tends to be higher in soft waters, since many of the iron compounds of soils and rocks are dissolved by the acidity of the waters. In many soft water areas, the differences between ground waters and surface waters are not as pronounced as in hard water regions, although many exceptions to this generality could be cited.

A more or less typical analysis of surface water in a region of generally insoluble soils and rocks follows:

Hardness	46	mg/l as $CaCO_3$
Calcium	30	mg/l as $CaCO_3$
Magnesium	16	mg/l as $CaCO_3$
Sodium & Potassium	9	mg/l as Na
Bicarbonate	42	mg/l as $CaCO_3$
Chloride	5	mg/l as Cl
Sulfate	12	mg/l as SO_4

Nitrate	1.5	mg/l as N
Iron	1.1	mg/l as Fe
Silica	30	mg/l as SiO_2

Ground water from a similar region might give analytical results similar to the following:

Hardness	61	mg/l as $CaCO_3$
Calcium	29	mg/l as $CaCO_3$
Magnesium	32	mg/l as $CaCO_3$
Sodium	26	mg/l as Na
Bicarbonate	60	mg/l as $CaCO_3$
Chloride	7	mg/l as Cl
Sulfate	17	mg/l as SO_4
Carbon Dioxide	59	mg/l as $CaCO_3$
PH	6.6	
Iron	1.8	mg/l as Fe

It is worth re-emphasizing that each of the constituents listed in the analyses above may vary over a wide range from place to place.

For example, waters are known with hardness values of less than 10 mg/l, and others have concentrations over 1,000 mg/l. Those quoted have been chosen to represent rather moderate, ordinary values occurring in two distinct types of situations common in the United States. It would be a mistake, however, to expect any water sample to correspond exactly to any one of the analyses given as examples.

Good Quality Water. Since waters from various sources may vary so markedly in composition, one may reasonably question which source should be considered most desirable. The problem has several practical consequences. For example, if a choice exists among several available sources, the final decision may rest upon judgment of their relative quality. Also, when the composition is modified by treatment, the objective is to approach, if not always to attain, the ideal.

The characteristics of "good quality water" are implied in earlier sections of this chapter, which discuss the objectives of water treatment and the standards formally adopted by the U.S. Public Health Service. Reviewing those sections will make it evident that the properties desired are mostly negative. That is, the objectives and standards are directed principally to avoiding undesirable qualities. The properties of " good" water may then be summarized in qualitative terms as follows:
1. Absence of harmful concentrations of poisonous chemical substances
2. Absence of the causative microorganisms and viruses of disease
3. Lowest possible levels of color, turbidity, suspended solids, odor, and taste
4. Lowest possible temperature
5. Minimum corrosivity to metals
6. Least possible tendency to deposit scale
7. Lowest possible content of staining materials, such as iron, manganese, and copper

This may appear to suggest that the ideal water contains the lowest possible quantity of total solids but this is not the case. Extremely soft waters tend to be excessively corrosive to metals, and many persons find them unpalatable. Moreover, they seem to be less effective in removing soap by rinsing than waters containing a little hardness.

Although there has been no formal recognition of a set of analytical values characterizing the "ideal" water, the following would probably be considered generally acceptable as an approximation:

Alkyl Benzene Sulfonate	less than 0.1 mg/l, preferably 0
Arsenic	less than 0.01 mg/l, preferably 0
Barium	less than 1 mg/l, preferably 0
Bicarbonate*	150 mg/l as $CaCO_3$
Cadium	less than 0.01 mg/l, preferably 0
Calcium*	70 mg/l as $CaCO_3$
Carbon Chloroform Extract	less than 0.2 mg/l, preferably 0
Carbon Dioxide*	6 mg/1 as $CaCO_3$
Chloride*	less than 250 mg/l, preferably 0
Chromium, Hexavalent	less than 0.05 mg/l, preferably 0
Coliform Bacteria	less than 1 per 100 ml
Color	less than 15 units, preferably 0
Copper	less than 1 mg/l, preferably 0
Cyanide	less than 0.01 mg/l, preferably 0
Fluoride	approximately 0.9 mg/l (somewhat dependent upon climate)
Hardness*	70 mg/l as $CaCO_3$
Iron	less than 0.1 mg/l, preferably 0
Lead	less than 0.05 mg/l, preferably 0
Magnesium*	preferably 0
Manganese	less than 0.02 mg/l, preferably 0
Nitrate	less than 10 mg/l, preferably 0
pH*	7.8
Phenols	less than 0.001 mg/l, preferably 0
Selenium	less than 0.01 mg/l, preferably 0
Silver	less than 0.05 mg/l, preferably 0
Sodium & Potassium*	37 mg/l as Na
Sulfate*	less than 250 mg/l, preferably 0
Suspended Solids	not detectable
Temperature	33 to 40 degrees Fahrenheit
Threshold Odor Number	less than 3, preferably 0
Total Dissolved Solids	less than 500 mg/l
Turbidity	less than 5 units, preferably 0
Zinc	less than 5 mg/l, preferably 0

*The relationships among calcium, bicarbonate, carbon dioxide, and pH should be such as to minimize scaling and corrosion. In some cases, these concentrations may dictate the most desirable concentrations of sulfate, chloride, magnesium, sodium, and potassium.

Self-Purification and Storage

Nature provides some degree of self-purification for all water that has been polluted or contaminated by the introduction of wastes, whether they originate as domestic sewage, industrial wastes, or drainage from yards, streets, and agricultural areas. The rate at which process occurs depends upon the nature and amount of polluting material as well as the physical, chemical, and biological conditions and characteristics of the water itself. Erroneous ideas are prevalent, however, particularly as to the value of aeration and its effect on flowing water. For instance, statements are sometimes made to the effect that "water will purify itself in flowing seven miles," or that natural aeration occurring at waterfalls and rapids will "oxidize" or kill bacteria. Actually, distance in itself has nothing whatever to do with self-purification in a flowing stream. Neither does aeration have much if any direct effect in killing bacteria. Time is the important factor, together wth proper conditions of temperature, sunlight, velocity of flow and many other complex chemical, physical, and biological characteristics. Quiescent sedimentation in a reservoir for a period of about a month may result generally in purification equivalent to that of filtration. Sluggish flow in a stream for a long distance may accomplish the same results.

The general appearance of a stream provides a useful guide to the degree of pollution. For instance, the bed of the unpolluted portion above sources of wastewaters usually is coated with a greenish brown deposit and green, rooted plants will thrive in protected areas. Just below a point of pollution, chemical and biological changes are evident, such as the gradual disappearance of the green plants. This stretch of the stream has been called the "zone of recent pollution."

Further downstream is the "zone of active decomposition", where the bed of the stream may have black sludge deposits, and a characteristic biological population adapted to a plentiful food supply but a limited oxygen supply. If the degree of pollution is great, the dissolved oxygen of the water may be completely exhausted. This results generally in objectionable conditions, the production of odors and gases, and a turbid gray or black appearance of the water. If, on the other hand, the degree of pollution is moderate and the dissolved oxygen content of the water is sufficient, odors are not produced. This condition results when the dissolved oxygen is replenished from the atmosphere and plant life at a rate faster than it is being used up in oxidation of the polluting material. The presence of rapids, falls, or even swiftly flowing water in this zone is helpful insofar as providing an adequate supply of atmospheric oxygen is concerned, since the rate of reaeration is closely related to the turbulence of the water. It should be noted, however, that a supply of oxygen exceeding the requirements does not accelerate the natural purification processes. Since the time is not shortened, a high flow velocity only means that the distance traveled before purification is complete is increased.

Eventually, unless additional pollution is discharged into the stream, the result is the production of an odorless, humus-like material in the stream bed. If the pollution contained nitrogenous materials, the concentration of nitrates in the water increases. There is restoration of the normal dissolved oxygen content, which favors the growth of green aquatic vegetation. Normal conditions are thus restored in this "zone of recovery," the length and position of which are dependent upon the degree of pollution and the natural conditions outlined above.

Essentially, the same action takes place in a natural lake or in an impounding reservoir, although the "zones" described above may not exist as distinct regions. This is due to the complications which are caused by the lack of currents with definite direction. Furthermore, a considerable amount of vertical mixing may occur due to variations in the density of the water. The changes of density, in turn, are caused by the differences of temperature of the water at the various levels in the lake or reservoir. The vertical mixing takes place continuously, but is most noticeable in the spring and fall when temperature changes are most rapid and mixing consequently most vigorous throughout the entire depth of the water. Very often this "turnover" of a lake or reservoir results in the occurrence of tastes and odors in the water supply, which may be due to changes in the types and numbers of microorganisms present, or to changes in the chemical and physical quality of the water.

In general, self-purification results in the removal of organic matter and the degree depends upon the dilution, the effectiveness of reaeration, sedimentation, and most important, the time interval available for biochemical action. The destruction of bacteria introduced with sewage, however, is controlled by a different set of factors. The rate is controlled by the water temperature, available food supply, the germicidal effect of sunlight, sedimentation, and the consumption of the bacteria as food by protozoa. This action is usually slower than the destruction of organic matter. Hence, bacterial contamination may persist long after the visible evidence of pollution has disappeared. Therefore, the only possible way of determining the influence of storage or of passage along a stream upon the bacteriological quality of the water is to measure bacterial numbers in representative samples of water collected at appropriate points.

Unfortunately, the effects of storage and time are not all beneficial in relation to certain characteristics of water. The results of biochemical purification are, for example, conductive to the growth of algae and other forms of microscopic plant and animal life. Although these organisms may have little if any effect on the health of a community as a result of drinking the water, they are the most common cause of tastes and odors, and generally, additional treatment is needed when they are present.

Methods of Water Treatment

The methods employed in the treatment of water depend, to a large extent, on the purpose for which the supply is to be used and the quality of the water being treated. For domestic use, it is desirable to remove any materials, either in suspension or in solution, which are detrimental to the appearance and esthetic appeal of the water. It is absolutely necessary to remove or kill any detrimental microorganisms, and to remove harmful chemical substances. On the other hand, industrial requirements for water quality vary, depending upon the use. For example, for stream generation the control of scale formation is of paramount importance, while textile mills and paper mills demand freedom from iron and manganese.

In general, the many methods normally employed in water treatment practice usually have as their main objective the reduction of the total quantity of foreign substances in the water. Even when the treatment process involves the addition of certain materials, the end result is usually the removal of more material than has been added. There are cases, however, in which certain constituents are removed by substituting other substances, and in some circumstances the content of certain substances may be increased deliberately, in order to impart certain desirable characteristics to the water.

Sedimentation. Sedimentation is more or less effective in the removal of suspended matter, depending upon the size and the density of the particles to be removed, and the time available for the process. Large or heavy particles are removed in a relatively short time, while a much longer period is required for light or finely divided materials. Some of the very finest such as eroded clay may not be removed even by several days' sedimentation. If the concentration of such "non-settleable" particles is excessive, then sedimentation alone is not an adequate method of treatment, and other means must be employed.

Coagulation. This is the technique of treating the water with certain chemicals for the purpose of collecting non-settleable particles into larger or heavier aggregates which are more readily removed. The resulting clumps of solid material, termed "floc," are removed by sedimentation, filtration, or both.

Filtration. Filtration of the water through sand, anthracite, diatomite, and other fine-grained materials is also capable of removing particulate matter too light or too finely divided to be removed by sedimentation. Filters often follow sedimentation units, so that the larger quantity of relatively coarse material is removed by sedimentation, to avoid rapid clogging of the filters, which in turn remove the particles for which sedimentation is not effective. Fine screens or microstrainers are sometimes used prior to sand filtration.

Disinfection. This broad sense means destroying pathogenic organisms. In the practice of water treatment in the United States, it is usually accomplished by the application of chlorine or certain chlorine compounds. Although many other treatment processes mentioned also have some effect upon the microbial population of the water, disinfection is the only step which is intended specifically for control of the bacteriological quality.

Softening. The removal of the elements which contribute hardness to a water supply, primarily calcium and magnesium is called softening. Many water supplies do not require softening, and in some cases, even though the water is hard, softening is not practiced. When domestic supplies are softened, usually the *lime-soda process* or the *ion-exchange process* is used. In the first, chemicals are added to precipitate calcium as calcium carbonate, and if further softening is required, magnesium is precipitated as magnesium hydroxide. Usually, the process results in a reduction of the total quantity of dissolved solids in the water. In the ion-exchange process, calcium and magnesium salts are converted to sodium salts, and little change in the total dissolved solids results.

Aeration. This may be used for a variety of purposes. Since volatile substances are removed in the process to some extent, and these may include materials which affect the taste and odor of the water, aeration is sometimes employed in connection with taste and odor control. Excessive carbon dioxide can also be removed in this way, and the corrosive effect of some water can be reduced. The removal of carbon dioxide by aeration sometimes also reduces the dosages of chemicals required in subsequent treatment processes. Finally, by supplying dissolved oxygen, aeration is often helpful in the removal of iron.

Iron and manganese removal. Specific processes to remove iron and manganese are employed only in waters which contain sufficient concentrations of these substances to cause persistent problems. A number of different techniques exist, and the choice depends upon the concentration and the chemical nature of the iron and manganese present.

Taste and odor removal. Taste and odor are affected by many of the treatment processes which are employed primarily for other purposes, and therefore, like some other characteristics, do not require special processes for control unless rather unusual problems exist. Which one of the several available processes proves to be most successful depends upon the nature and the concentration of the offending substances. It has been mentioned that some odors are effectively removed by aeration. Others may require either adsorption or oxidation for efficient control.

Corrosion control. This is accomplished in some cases by the removal of excess carbon dioxide (e.g., by aeration). In other cases, alkalinity is added to the water in the form of an alkaline chemical such as sodium carbonate.

Fluoridation. The objective of this process is to attain a concentration of fluoride in the water which imparts to the population the maximum degree of resistance to tooth decay.

PHILOSOPHY, PRINCIPLES, PRACTICES, AND TECHNICS
OF
SUPERVISION, ADMINISTRATION, MANAGEMENT, AND ORGANIZATION

TABLE OF CONTENTS

	Page
MEANING OF SUPERVISION	1
THE OLD AND THE NEW SUPERVISION	1
THE EIGHT (8) BASIC PRINCIPLES OF THE NEW SUPERVISION	1
I. Principle of Responsibility	1
II. Principle of Authority	2
III. Principle of Self-Growth	2
IV. Principle of Individual Worth	2
V. Principle of Creative Leadership	2
VI. Principle of Success and Failure	2
VII. Principle of Science	3
VIII. Principle of Cooperation	3
WHAT IS ADMINISTRATION?	3
I. Practices Commonly Classed as "Supervisory"	3
II. Practices Commonly Classed as "Administrative"	3
III. Practices Commonly Classed as Both "Supervisory" and "Administrative"	4
RESPONSIBILITIES OF THE SUPERVISOR	4
COMPETENCIES OF THE SUPERVISOR	4
THE PROFESSIONAL SUPERVISOR-EMPLOYEE RELATIONSHIP	4
MINI-TEXT IN SUPERVISION, ADMINISTRATION, MANAGEMENT, AND ORGANIZATION	5
I. Brief Highlights	5
A. Levels of Management	6
B. What the Supervisor Must Learn	6
C. A Definition of Supervision	6
D. Elements of the Team Concept	6
E. Principles of Organization	6
F. The Four Important Parts of Every Job	7
G. Principles of Delegation	7
H. Principles of Effective Communications	7
I. Principles of Work Improvement	7
J. Areas of Job Improvement	7
K. Seven Key Points in Making Improvements	8

	L.	Corrective Techniques for Job Improvement	8
	M.	A Planning Checklist	8
	N.	Five Characteristics of Good Directions	9
	O.	Types of Directions	9
	P.	Controls	9
	Q.	Orienting the New Employee	9
	R.	Checklist for Orienting New Employees	9
	S.	Principles of Learning	10
	T.	Causes of Poor Performance	10
	U.	Four Major Steps in On-the-Job Instructions	10
	V.	Employees Want Five Things	10
	W.	Some Don'ts in Regard to Praise	11
	X.	How to Gain Your Workers' Confidence	11
	Y.	Sources of Employee Problems	11
	Z.	The Supervisor's Key to Discipline	11
	AA.	Five Important Processes of Management	12
	BB.	When the Supervisor Fails to Plan	12
	CC.	Fourteen General Principles of Management	12
	DD.	Change	12
II.	Brief Topical Summaries		13
	A.	Who/What is the Supervisor?	13
	B.	The Sociology of Work	13
	C.	Principles and Practices of Supervision	14
	D.	Dynamic Leadership	14
	E.	Processes for Solving Problems	15
	F.	Training for Results	15
	G.	Health, Safety, and Accident Prevention	16
	H.	Equal Employment Opportunity	16
	I.	Improving Communications	16
	J.	Self-Development	17
	K.	Teaching and Training	17
		1. The Teaching Process	17
		a. Preparation	17
		b. Presentation	18
		c. Summary	18
		d. Application	18
		e. Evaluation	18
		2. Teaching Methods	18
		a. Lecture	18
		b. Discussion	18
		c. Demonstration	19
		d. Performance	19
		e. Which Method to Use	19

PHILOSOPHY, PRINCIPLES, PRACTICES, AND TECHNICS OF SUPERVISION, ADMINISTRATION, MANAGEMENT, AND ORGANIZATION

MEANING OF SUPERVISION

The extension of the democratic philosophy has been accompanied by an extension in the scope of supervision. Modern leaders and supervisors no longer think of supervision in the narrow sense of being confined chiefly to visiting employees, supplying materials, or rating the staff. They regard supervision as being intimately related to all the concerned agencies of society, they speak of the supervisor's function in terms of "growth," rather than the "improvement" of employees.

This modern concept of supervision may be defined as follows: Supervision is leadership and the development of leadership within groups which are cooperatively engaged in inspection, research, training, guidance, and evaluation.

THE OLD AND THE NEW SUPERVISION

TRADITIONAL
1. Inspection
2. Focused on the employee
3. Visitation
4. Random and haphazard
5. Imposed and authoritarian
6. One person usually

MODERN
1. Study and analysis
2. Focused on aims, materials, methods, supervisors, employees, environment
3. Demonstrations, intervisitation, workshops, directed reading, bulletins, etc.
4. Definitely organized and planned (scientific)
5. Cooperative and democratic
6. Many persons involved (creative)

THE EIGHT (8) BASIC PRINCIPLES OF THE NEW SUPERVISION

I. Principle of Responsibility
   Authority to act and responsibility for acting must be joined.
   A. If you give responsibility, give authority.
   B. Define employee duties clearly.
   C. Protect employees from criticism by others.
   D. Recognize the rights as well as obligations of employees.
   E. Achieve the aims of a democratic society insofar as it is possible within the area of your work.
   F. Establish a situation favorable to training and learning.
   G. Accept ultimate responsibility for everything done in your section, unit, office, division, department.
   H. Good administration and good supervision are inseparable.

II. Principle of Authority
The success of the supervisor is measured by the extent to which the power of authority is not used.
   A. Exercise simplicity and informality in supervision
   B. Use the simplest machinery of supervision
   C. If it is good for the organization as a whole, it is probably justified.
   D. Seldom be arbitrary or authoritative.
   E. Do not base your work on the power of position or of personality.
   F. Permit and encourage the free expression of opinions.

III. Principle of Self-Growth
The success of the supervisor is measured by the extent to which, and the speed with which, he is no longer needed.
   A. Base criticism on principles, not on specifics.
   B. Point out higher activities to employees.
   C. Train for self-thinking by employees to meet new situations.
   D. Stimulate initiative, self-reliance, and individual responsibility
   E. Concentrate on stimulating the growth of employees rather than on removing defects.

IV. Principle of Individual Worth
Respect for the individual is a paramount consideration in supervision.
   A. Be human and sympathetic in dealing with employees.
   B. Don't nag about things to be done.
   C. Recognize the individual differences among employees and seek opportunities to permit best expression of each personality.

V. Principle of Creative Leadership
The best supervision is that which is not apparent to the employee.
   A. Stimulate, don't drive employees to creative action.
   B. Emphasize doing good things.
   C. Encourage employees to do what they do best.
   D. Do not be too greatly concerned with details of subject or method.
   E. Do not be concerned exclusively with immediate problems and activities.
   F. Reveal higher activities and make them both desired and maximally possible.
   G. Determine procedures in the light of each situation but see that these are derived from a sound basic philosophy.
   H. Aid, inspire, and lead so as to liberate the creative spirit latent in all good employees.

VI. Principle of Success and Failure
There are no unsuccessful employees, only unsuccessful supervisors who have failed to give proper leadership.
   A. Adapt suggestions to the capacities, attitudes, and prejudices of employees.
   B. Be gradual, be progressive, be persistent.
   C. Help the employee find the general principle; have the employee apply his own problem to the general principle.
   D. Give adequate appreciation for good work and honest effort.
   E. Anticipate employee difficulties and help to prevent them.
   F. Encourage employees to do the desirable things they will do anyway.
   G. Judge your supervision by the results it secures.

VII. Principle of Science
Successful supervision is scientific, objective, and experimental. It is based on facts, not on prejudices.
   A. Be cumulative in results.
   B. Never divorce your suggestions from the goals of training.
   C. Don't be impatient of results.
   D. Keep all matters on a professional, not a personal, level.
   E. Do not be concerned exclusively with immediate problems and activities.
   F. Use objective means of determining achievement and rating where possible.

VIII. Principle of Cooperation
Supervision is a cooperative enterprise between supervisor and employee.
   A. Begin with conditions as they are.
   B. Ask opinions of all involved when formulating policies.
   C. Organization is as good as its weakest link.
   D. Let employees help to determine policies and department programs.
   E. Be approachable and accessible—physically and mentally.
   F. Develop pleasant social relationships.

WHAT IS ADMINISTRATION

Administration is concerned with providing the environment, the material facilities, and the operational procedures that will promote the maximum growth and development of supervisors and employees. (Organization is an aspect and a concomitant of administration.)

There is no sharp line of demarcation between supervision and administration; these functions are intimately interrelated and, often, overlapping. They are complementary activities.

I. Practices Commonly Classed as "Supervisory"
   A. Conducting employees' conferences
   B. Visiting sections, units, offices, divisions, departments
   C. Arranging for demonstrations
   D. Examining plans
   E. Suggesting professional reading
   F. Interpreting bulletins
   G. Recommending in-service training courses
   H. Encouraging experimentation
   I. Appraising employee morale
   J. Providing for intervisitation

II. Practices Commonly Classified as "Administrative"
   A. Management of the office
   B. Arrangement of schedules for extra duties
   C. Assignment of rooms or areas
   D. Distribution of supplies
   E. Keeping records and reports
   F. Care of audio-visual materials
   G. Keeping inventory records
   H. Checking record cards and books

4

    I. Programming special activities
    J. Checking on the attendance and punctuality of employees

III. Practices Commonly Classified as Both "Supervisory" and "Administrative"
    A. Program construction
    B. Testing or evaluating outcomes
    C. Personnel accounting
    D. Ordering instructional materials

RESPONSIBILITIES OF THE SUPERVISOR

A person employed in a supervisory capacity must constantly be able to improve his own efficiency and ability. He represent the employer to the employees and only continuous self-examination can make him a capable supervisor.

Leadership and training are the supervisor's responsibility. An efficient working unit is one in which the employees work with the supervisor. It is his job to bring out the best in his employees. He must always be relaxed, courteous, and calm in his association with his employees. Their feelings are important, and a harsh attitude does not develop the most efficient employees.

COMPETENCES OF THE SUPERVISOR

    I. Complete knowledge of the duties and responsibilities of his position.
    II. To be able to organize a job, plan ahead, and carry through.
    III. To have self-confidence and initiative.
    IV. To be able to handle the unexpected situation and make quick decisions.
    V. To be able to properly train subordinates in the positions they are best suited for.
    VI. To be able to keep good human relations among his subordinates.
    VII. To be able to keep good human relations between his subordinates and himself and to earn their respect and trust.

THE PROFESSIONAL SUPERVISOR-EMPLOYEE RELATIONSHIP

There are two kinds of efficiency: one kind is only apparent and is produced in organizations through the exercise of mere discipline; this is but a simulation of the second, or true, efficiency which springs from spontaneous cooperation. If you are a manager, no matter how great or small your responsibility, it is your job, in the final analysis, to create and develop this involuntary cooperation among the people whom you supervise. For, no matter how powerful a combination of money, machines, and materials a company may have, this is a dead and sterile thing without a team of willing, thinking, and articulate people to guide it.

The following 21 points are presented as indicative of the exemplary basic relationship that should exist between supervisor and employee:

1. Each person wants to be liked and respected by his fellow employee and wants to be treated with consideration and respect by his superior.
2. The most competent employee will make an error. However, in a unit where good relations exist between the supervisor and his employees, tenseness and fear do not exist. Thus, errors are not hidden or covered up, and the efficiency of a unit is not impaired.

3. Subordinates resent rules, regulations, or orders that are unreasonable or unexplained.
4. Subordinates are quick to resent unfairness, harshness, injustices, and favoritism.
5. An employee will accept responsibility if he knows that he will be complimented for a job well done, and not too harshly chastised for failure; that his supervisor will check the cause of the failure, and, if it was the supervisor's fault, he will assume the blame therefore. If it was the employee's fault, his supervisor will explain the correct method or means of handling the responsibility.
6. An employee wants to receive credit for a suggestion he has made, that is used. If a suggestion cannot be used, the employee is entitled to an explanation. The supervisor should not say "no" and close the subject.
7. Fear and worry slow up a worker's ability. Poor working environment can impair his physical and mental health. A good supervisor avoids forceful methods, threats, and arguments to get a job done.
8. A forceful supervisor is able to train his employees individually and as a team, and is able to motivate them in the proper channels.
9. A mature supervisor is able to properly evaluate his subordinates and to keep them happy and satisfied.
10. A sensitive supervisor will never patronize his subordinates.
11. A worthy supervisor will respect his employees' confidences.
12. Definite and clear-cut responsibilities should be assigned to each executive.
13. Responsibility should always be coupled with corresponding authority.
14. No change should be made in the scope or responsibilities of a position without a definite understanding to that effect on the part of all persons concerned.
15. No executive or employee, occupying a single position in the organization, should be subject to definite orders from more than one source.
16. Orders should never be given to subordinates over the head of a responsible executive. Rather than do this, the officer in question should be supplanted.
17. Criticisms of subordinates should, whoever possible, be made privately, and in no case should a subordinate be criticized in the presence of executives or employees of equal or lower rank.
18. No dispute or difference between executives or employees as to authority or responsibilities should be considered too trivial for prompt and careful adjudication.
19. Promotions, wage changes, and disciplinary action should always be approved by the executive immediately superior to the one directly responsible.
20. No executive or employee should ever be required, or expected, to be at the same time an assistant to, and critic of, another.
21. Any executive whose work is subject to regular inspection should, wherever practicable, be given the assistance and facilities necessary to enable him to maintain an independent check of the quality of his work.

MINI-TEXT IN SUPERVISION, ADMINISTRATION, MANAGEMENT, AND ORGANIZATION

I. Brief Highlights

Listed concisely and sequentially are major headings and important data in the field for quick recall and review.

A. Levels of Management
   Any organization of some size has several levels of management. In terms of a ladder, the levels are:

   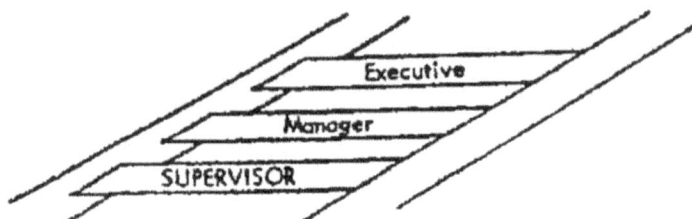

   The first level is very important because it is the beginning point of management leadership.

B. What the Supervisor Must Learn
   A supervisor must learn to:
   1. Deal with people and their differences
   2. Get the job done through people
   3. Recognize the problems when they exist
   4. Overcome obstacles to good performance
   5. Evaluate the performance of people
   6. Check his own performance in terms of accomplishment

C. A Definition of Supervisor
   The term supervisor means any individual having authority, in the interests of the employer, to hire, transfer, suspend, lay-off, recall, promote, discharge, assign, reward, or discipline other employees or responsibility to direct them, or to adjust their grievances, or effectively to recommend such action, if, in connection with the foregoing, exercise of such authority is not of a merely routine or clerical nature but requires the use of independent judgment.

D. Elements of the Team Concept
   What is involved in teamwork? The component parts are:
   1. Members
   2. A leader
   3. Goals
   4. Plans
   5. Cooperation
   6. Spirit

E. Principles of Organization
   1. A team member must know what his job is.
   2. Be sure that the nature and scope of a job are understood.
   3. Authority and responsibility should be carefully spelled out.
   4. A supervisor should be permitted to make the maximum number of decisions affecting his employees.
   5. Employees should report to only one supervisor.
   6. A supervisor should direct only as many employees as he can handle effectively.
   7. An organization plan should be flexible.

8. Inspection and performance of work should be separate.
9. Organizational problems should receive immediate attention.
10. Assign work in line with ability and experience.

F. The Four Important Parts of Every Job
1. Inherent in every job is the *accountability* for results.
2. A second set of factors in every job is *responsibilities*.
3. Along with duties and responsibilities one must have the *authority* to act within certain limits without obtaining permission to proceed.
4. No job exists in a vacuum. The supervisor is surrounded by key *relationships*.

G. Principles of Delegation
Where work is delegated for the first time, the supervisor should think in terms of these questions:
1. Who is best qualified to do this?
2. Can an employee improve his abilities by doing this?
3. How long should an employee spend on this?
4. Are there any special problems for which he will need guidance?
5. How broad a delegation can I make?

H. Principles of Effective Communications
1. Determine the media.
2. To whom directed?
3. Identification and source authority.
4. Is communication understood?

I. Principles of Work Improvement
1. Most people usually do only the work which is assigned to them.
2. Workers are likely to fit assigned work into the time available to perform it.
3. A good workload usually stimulates output.
4. People usually do their best work when they know that results will be reviewed or inspected.
5. Employees usually feel that someone else is responsible for conditions of work, workplace layout, job methods, type of tools/equipment, and other such factors.
6. Employees are usually defensive about their job security.
7. Employees have natural resistance to change.
8. Employees can support or destroy a supervisor.
9. A supervisor usually earns the respect of his people through his personal example of diligence and efficiency.

J. Areas of Job Improvement
The areas of job improvement are quite numerous, but the most common ones which a supervisor can identify and utilize are:
1. Departmental layout
2. Flow of work
3. Workplace layout
4. Utilization of manpower
5. Work methods
6. Materials handling

7. Utilization
8. Motion economy

K. Seven Key Points in Making Improvements
1. Select the job to be improved
2. Study how it is being done now
3. Question the present method
4. Determine actions to be taken
5. Chart proposed method
6. Get approval and apply
7. Solicit worker participation

L. Corrective Techniques of Job Improvement
Specific Problems
1. Size of workload
2. Inability to meet schedules
3. Strain and fatigue
4. Improper use of men and skills
5. Waste, poor quality, unsafe conditions
6. Bottleneck conditions that hinder output
7. Poor utilization of equipment and machine
8. Efficiency and productivity of labor

General Improvement
1. Departmental layout
2. Flow of work
3. Work plan layout
4. Utilization of manpower
5. Work methods
6. Materials handling
7. Utilization of equipment
8. Motion economy

Corrective Techniques
1. Study with scale model
2. Flow chart study
3. Motion analysis
4. Comparison of units produced to standard allowance
5. Methods analysis
6. Flow chart and equipment study
7. Down time vs. running time
8. Motion analysis

M. A Planning Checklist
1. Objectives
2. Controls
3. Delegations
4. Communications
5. Resources
6. Manpower

7. Equipment
8. Supplies and materials
9. Utilization of time
10. Safety
11. Money
12. Work
13. Timing of improvements

N. Five Characteristics of Good Directions
In order to get results, directions must be:
1. Possible of accomplishment
2. Agreeable with worker interests
3. Related to mission
4. Planned and complete
5. Unmistakably clear

O. Types of Directions
1. Demands or direct orders
2. Requests
3. Suggestion or implication
4. volunteering

P. Controls
A typical listing of the overall areas in which the supervisor should establish controls might be:
1. Manpower
2. Materials
3. Quality of work
4. Quantity of work
5. Time
6. Space
7. Money
8. Methods

Q. Orienting the New Employee
1. Prepare for him
2. Welcome the new employee
3. Orientation for the job
4. Follow-up

R. Checklist for Orienting New Employees   Yes   No
1. Do you appreciate the feelings of new employees when they first report for work? ___ ___
2. Are you aware of the fact that the new employee must make a big adjustment to his job? ___ ___
3. Have you given him good reasons for liking the job and the organization? ___ ___
4. Have you prepared for his first day on the job? ___ ___
5. Did you welcome him cordially and make him feel needed? ___ ___

	Yes	No

6. Did you establish rapport with him so that he feels free to talk and discuss matters with you? ___ ___
7. Did you explain his job to him and his relationship to you? ___ ___
8. Does he know that his work will be evaluated periodically on a basis that is fair and objective? ___ ___
9. Did you introduce him to his fellow workers in such a way that they are likely to accept him? ___ ___
10. Does he know what employee benefits he will receive? ___ ___
11. Does he understand the importance of being on the job and what to do if he must leave his duty station? ___ ___
12. Has he been impressed with the importance of accident prevention and safe practice? ___ ___
13. Does he generally know his way around the department? ___ ___
14. Is he under the guidance of a sponsor who will teach the right way of doing things? ___ ___
15. Do you plan to follow-up so that he will continue to adjust successfully to his job? ___ ___

S. Principles of Learning
1. Motivation
2. Demonstration or explanation
3. Practice

T. Causes of Poor Performance
1. Improper training for job
2. Wrong tools
3. Inadequate directions
4. Lack of supervisory follow-up
5. Poor communications
6. Lack of standards of performance
7. Wrong work habits
8. Low morale
9. Other

U. Four Major Steps in On-The-Job Instruction
1. Prepare the worker
2. Present the operation
3. Tryout performance
4. Follow-up

V. Employees Want Five Things
1. Security
2. Opportunity
3. Recognition
4. Inclusion
5. Expression

W. Some Don'ts in Regard to Praise
1. Don't praise a person for something he hasn't done.
2. Don't praise a person unless you can be sincere.
3. Don't be sparing in praise just because your superior withholds it from you.
4. Don't let too much time elapse between good performance and recognition of it

X. How to Gain Your Workers' Confidence
Methods of developing confidence include such things as:
1. Knowing the interests, habits, hobbies of employees
2. Admitting your own inadequacies
3. Sharing and telling of confidence in others
4. Supporting people when they are in trouble
5. Delegating matters that can be well handled
6. Being frank and straightforward about problems and working conditions
7. Encouraging others to bring their problems to you
8. Taking action on problems which impede worker progress

Y. Sources of Employee Problems
On-the-job causes might be such things as:
1. A feeling that favoritism is exercised in assignments
2. Assignment of overtime
3. An undue amount of supervision
4. Changing methods or systems
5. Stealing of ideas or trade secrets
6. Lack of interest in job
7. Threat of reduction in force
8. Ignorance or lack of communications
9. Poor equipment
10. Lack of knowing how supervisor feels toward employee
11. Shift assignments

Off-the-job problems might have to do with:
1. Health
2. Finances
3. Housing
4. Family

Z. The Supervisor's Key to Discipline
There are several key points about discipline which the supervisor should keep in mind:
1. Job discipline is one of the disciplines of life and is directed by the supervisor.
2. It is more important to correct an employee fault than to fix blame for it.
3. Employee performance is affected by problems both on the job and off.
4. Sudden or abrupt changes in behavior can be indications of important employee problems.
5. Problems should be dealt with as soon as possible after they are identified.
6. The attitude of the supervisor may have more to do with solving problems than the techniques of problem solving.
7. Correction of employee behavior should be resorted to only after the supervisor is sure that training or counseling will not be helpful.

8. Be sure to document your disciplinary actions.
9. Make sure that you are disciplining on the basis of facts rather than personal feelings.
10. Take each disciplinary step in order, being careful not to make snap judgments, or decisions based on impatience.

AA. Five Important Processes of Management
1. Planning
2. Organizing
3. Scheduling
4. Controlling
5. Motivating

BB. When the Supervisor Fails to Plan
1. Supervisor creates impression of not knowing his job
2. May lead to excessive overtime
3. Job runs itself—supervisor lacks control
4. Deadlines and appointments missed
5. Parts of the work go undone
6. Work interrupted by emergencies
7. Sets a bad example
8. Uneven workload creates peaks and valleys
9. Too much time on minor details at expense of more important tasks

CC. Fourteen General Principles of Management
1. Division of work
2. Authority and responsibility
3. Discipline
4. Unity of command
5. Unity of direction
6. Subordination of individual interest to general interest
7. Remuneration of personnel
8. Centralization
9. Scalar chain
10. Order
11. Equity
12. Stability of tenure of personnel
13. Initiative
14. Esprit de corps

DD. Change

Bringing about change is perhaps attempted more often, and yet less well understood, than anything else the supervisor does. How do people generally react to change? (People tend to resist change that is imposed upon them by other individuals or circumstances.

Change is characteristic of every situation. It is a part of every real endeavor where the efforts of people are concerned.

1. Why do people resist change?
   People may resist change because of:
   a. Fear of the unknown
   b. Implied criticism
   c. Unpleasant experiences in the past
   d. Fear of loss of status
   e. Threat to the ego
   f. Fear of loss of economic stability

2. How can we best overcome the resistance to change?
   In initiating change, take these steps:
   a. Get ready to sell
   b. Identify sources of help
   c. Anticipate objections
   d. Sell benefits
   e. Listen in depth
   f. Follow up

II. Brief Topical Summaries

   A. Who/What is the Supervisor?
   1. The supervisor is often called the "highest level employee and the lowest level manager."
   2. A supervisor is a member of both management and the work group. He acts as a bridge between the two.
   3. Most problems in supervision are in the area of human relations, or people problems.
   4. Employees expect: Respect, opportunity to learn and to advance, and a sense of belonging, and so forth.
   5. Supervisors are responsible for directing people and organizing work. Planning is of paramount importance.
   6. A position description is a set of duties and responsibilities inherent to a given position.
   7. It is important to keep the position description up-to-date and to provide each employee with his own copy.

   B. The Sociology of Work
   1. People are alike in many ways; however, each individual is unique.
   2. The supervisor is challenged in getting to know employee differences. Acquiring skills in evaluating individuals is an asset.
   3. Maintaining meaningful working relationships in the organization is of great importance.
   4. The supervisor has an obligation to help individuals to develop to their fullest potential.
   5. Job rotation on a planned basis helps to build versatility and to maintain interest and enthusiasm in work groups.
   6. Cross training (job rotation) provides backup skills.

7. The supervisor can help reduce tension by maintaining a sense of humor, providing guidance to employees, and by making reasonable and timely decisions. Employees respond favorably to working under reasonably predictable circumstances.
8. Change is characteristic of all managerial behavior. The supervisor must adjust to changes in procedures, new methods, technological changes, and to a number of new and sometimes challenging situations.
9. To overcome the natural tendency for people to resist change, the supervisor should become more skillful in initiating change.

C. Principles and Practices of Supervision
1. Employees should be required to answer to only one superior.
2. A supervisor can effectively direct only a limited number of employees, depending upon the complexity, variety, and proximity of the jobs involved.
3. The organizational chart presents the organization in graphic form. It reflects lines of authority and responsibility as well as interrelationships of units within the organization.
4. Distribution of work can be improved through an analysis using the "Work Distribution Chart."
5. The "Work Distribution Chart" reflects the division of work within a unit in understandable form.
6. When related tasks are given to an employee, he has a better chance of increasing his skills through training.
7. The individual who is given the responsibility for tasks must also be given the appropriate authority to insure adequate results.
8. The supervisor should delegate repetitive, routine work. Preparation of recurring reports, maintaining leave and attendance records are some examples.
9. Good discipline is essential to good task performance. Discipline is reflected in the actions of employees on the job in the absence of supervision.
10. Disciplinary action may have to be taken when the positive aspects of discipline have failed. Reprimand, warning, and suspension are examples of disciplinary action.
11. If a situation calls for a reprimand, be sure it is deserved and remember it is to be done in private.

D. Dynamic Leadership
1. A style is a personal method or manner of exerting influence.
2. Authoritarian leaders often see themselves as the source of power and authority.
3. The democratic leader often perceives the group as the source of authority and power.
4. Supervisors tend to do better when using the pattern of leadership that is most natural for them.
5. Social scientists suggest that the effective supervisor use the leadership style that best fits the problem or circumstances involved.
6. All four styles—telling, selling, consulting, joining—have their place. Using one does not preclude using the other at another time.

7. The theory X point of view assumes that the average person dislikes work, will avoid it whenever possible, and must be coerced to achieve organizational objectives.
8. The theory Y point of view assumes that the average person considers work to be a natural as play, and, when the individual is committed, he requires little supervision or direction to accomplish desired objectives.
9. The leader's basic assumptions concerning human behavior and human nature affect his actions, decisions, and other managerial practices.
10. Dissatisfaction among employees is often present, but difficult to isolate. The supervisor should seek to weaken dissatisfaction by keeping promises, being sincere and considerate, keeping employees informed, and so forth.
11. Constructive suggestions should be encouraged during the natural progress of the work.

E. Processes for Solving Problems
 1. People find their daily tasks more meaningful and satisfying when they can improve them.
 2. The causes of problems, or the key factors, are often hidden in the background. Ability to solve problems often involves the ability to isolate them from their backgrounds. There is some substance to the cliché that some persons "can't see the forest for the trees."
 3. New procedures are often developed from old ones. Problems should be broken down into manageable parts. New ideas can be adapted from old one.
 4. People think differently in problem-solving situations. Using a logical, patterned approach is often useful. One approach found to be useful includes these steps:
    a. Define the problem
    b. Establish objectives
    c. Get the facts
    d. Weigh and decide
    e. Take action
    f. Evaluate action

F. Training for Results
 1. Participants respond best when they feel training is important to them.
 2. The supervisor has responsibility for the training and development of those who report to him.
 3. When training is delegated to others, great care must be exercised to insure the trainer has knowledge, aptitude, and interest for his work as a trainer.
 4. Training (learning) of some type goes on continually. The most successful supervisor makes certain the learning contributes in a productive manner to operational goals.
 5. New employees are particularly susceptible to training. Older employees facing new job situations require specific training, as well as having need for development and growth opportunities.
 6. Training needs require continuous monitoring.
 7. The training officer of an agency is a professional with a responsibility to assist supervisors in solving training problems.

8. Many of the self-development steps important to the supervisor's own growth are equally important to the development of peers and subordinates. Knowledge of these is important when the supervisor consults with others on development and growth opportunities.

G. Health, Safety, and Accident Prevention
1. Management-minded supervisors take appropriate measures to assist employees in maintaining health and in assuring safe practices in the work environment.
2. Effective safety training and practices help to avoid injury and accidents.
3. Safety should be a management goal. All infractions of safety which are observed should be corrected without exception.
4. Employees' safety attitude, training and instruction, provision of safe tools and equipment, supervision, and leadership are considered highly important factors which contribute to safety and which can be influenced directly by supervisors.
5. When accidents do occur, they should be investigated promptly for very important reasons, including the fact that information which is gained can be used to prevent accidents in the future.

H. Equal Employment Opportunity
1. The supervisor should endeavor to treat all employees fairly, without regard to religion, race, sex, or national origin.
2. Groups tend to reflect the attitude of the leader. Prejudice can be detected even in very subtle form. Supervisors must strive to create a feeling of mutual respect and confidence in every employee.
3. Complete utilization of all human resources is a national goal. Equitable consideration should be accorded women in the work force, minority-group members, the physically and mentally handicapped, and the older employee. The important question is: "Who can do the job?"
4. Training opportunities, recognition for performance, overtime assignments, promotional opportunities, and all other personnel actions are to be handled on an equitable basis.

I. Improving Communications
1. Communications is achieving understanding between the sender and the receiver of a message. It also means sharing information—the creation of understanding.
2. Communication is basic to all human activity. Words are means of conveying meanings; however, real meanings are in people.
3. There are very practical differences in the effectiveness of one-way, impersonal, and two-way communications. Words spoken face-to-face are better understood. Telephone conversations are effective, but lack the rapport of person-to-person exchanges. The whole person communicates.
4. Cooperation and communication in an organization go hand in hand. When there is a mutual respect between people, spelling out rules and procedures for communicating is unnecessary.
5. There are several barriers to effective communications. These include failure to listen with respect and understanding, lack of skill in feedback, and misinterpreting the meanings of words used by the speaker. It is also common

practice to listen to what we want to hear, and tune out things we do not want to hear.
6. Communication is management's chief problem. The supervisor should accept the challenge to communicate more effectively and to improve interagency and intra-agency communications.
7. The supervisor may often plan for and conduct meetings. The planning phase is critical and may determine the success or the failure of a meeting.
8. Speaking before groups usually requires extra effort. Stage fright may never disappear completely, but it can be controlled.

J. Self-Development
1. Every employee is responsible for his own self-development.
2. Toastmaster and toastmistress clubs offer opportunities to improve skills in oral communications.
3. Planning for one's own self-development is of vital importance. Supervisors know their own strengths and limitations better than anyone else.
4. Many opportunities are open to aid the supervisor in his developmental efforts, including job assignments; training opportunities, both governmental and non-governmental—to include universities and professional conferences and seminars.
5. Programmed instruction offers a means of studying at one's own rate.
6. Where difficulties may arise from a supervisor's being away from his work for training, he may participate in televised home study or correspondence courses to meet his self-development needs.

K. Teaching and Training
1. The Teaching Process
Teaching is encouraging and guiding the learning activities of students toward established goals. In most cases this process consists of five steps: preparation, presentation, summarization, evaluation, and application.

   a. Preparation
   Preparation is two-fold in nature; that of the supervisor and the employee. Preparation by the supervisor is absolutely essential to success. He must know what, when, where, how, and whom he will teach. Some of the factors that should be considered are:
   1) The objectives
   2) The materials needed
   3) The methods to be used
   4) Employee participation
   5) Employee interest
   6) Training aids
   7) Evaluation
   8) Summarization

   Employee preparation consists in preparing the employee to receive the material. Probably the most important single factor in the preparation of the employee is arousing and maintaining his interest. He must know the objectives of the training, why he is there, how the material can be used, and its importance to him.

b. Presentation
In presentation, have a carefully designed plan and follow it. The plan should be accurate and complete, yet flexible enough to meet situations as they arise. The method of presentation will be determined by the particular situation and objectives.

c. Summary
A summary should be made at the end of every training unit and program. In addition, there may be internal summaries depending on the nature of the material being taught. The important thing is that the trainee must always be able to understand how each part of the new material relates to the whole.

d. Application
The supervisor must arrange work so the employee will be given a chance to apply new knowledge or skills while the material is still clear in his mind and interest is high. The trainee does not really know whether he has learned the material until he has been given a chance to apply it. If the material is not applied, it loses most of its value.

e. Evaluation
The purpose of all training is to promote learning. To determine whether the training has been a success or failure, the supervisor must evaluate this learning.
In the broadest sense, evaluation includes all the devices, methods, skills, and techniques used by the supervisor to keep himself and the employees informed as to their progress toward the objectives they are pursuing. The extent to which the employee has mastered the knowledge, skills, and abilities, or changed his attitudes, as determined by the program objectives, is the extent to which instruction has succeeded or failed.
Evaluation should not be confined to the end of the lesson, day, or program but should be used continuously. We shall note later the way this relates to the rest of the teaching process.

2. Teaching Methods
A teaching method is a pattern of identifiable student and instructor activity used in presenting training material.
All supervisors are faced with the problem of deciding which method should be used at a given time.

a. Lecture
The lecture is direct oral presentation of material by the supervisor. The present trend is to place less emphasis on the trainer's activity and more on that of the trainee.

b. Discussion
Teaching by discussion or conference involves using questions and other techniques to arouse interest and focus attention upon certain areas, and by doing so creating a learning situation. This can be one of the most

valuable methods because it gives the employees an opportunity to express their ideas and pool their knowledge.

c. Demonstration
The demonstration is used to teach how something works or how to do something. It can be used to show a principle or what the results of a series of actions will be. A well-staged demonstration is particularly effective because it shows proper methods of performance in a realistic manner.

d. Performance
Performance is one of the most fundamental of all learning techniques or teaching methods. The trainee may be able to tell how a specific operation should be performed but he cannot be sure he knows how to perform the operation until he has done so.
As with all methods, there are certain advantages and disadvantages to each method.

e. Which Method to Use
Moreover, there are other methods and techniques of teaching. It is difficult to use any method without other methods entering into it. In any learning situation, a combination of methods is usually more effective than any one method alone.

Finally, evaluation must be integrated into the other aspects of the teaching-learning process.

It must be used in the motivation of the trainees; it must be used to assist in developing understanding during the training; and it must be related to employee application of the results of training.

This is distinctly the role of the supervisor.

www.ingramcontent.com/pod-product-compliance
Lightning Source LLC
Chambersburg PA
CBHW081824300426
44116CB00014B/2471